Innovation + Equality

Innovation + Equality

How to Create a Future That Is More *Star Trek* Than *Terminator*

Joshua Gans and Andrew Leigh

Foreword by Lawrence H. Summers

The MIT Press
Cambridge, Massachusetts
London, England

This book was set in Stone Serif and Stone Sans by Westchester Publishing Services. Printed and bound in the United States of America.

Library of Congress Cataloging-in-Publication Data

Names: Gans, Joshua, 1968- author. | Leigh, Andrew, 1972- author.
Title: Innovation + equality : how to create a future that is more star trek
   than terminator / Joshua Gans and Andrew Leigh ; foreword by Lawrence H.
   Summers.
Other titles: Innovation plus equality
Description: Cambridge, MA : MIT Press, [2019] | Includes bibliographical
   references and index.
Identifiers: LCCN 2019005650 | ISBN 9780262043229 (hardcover : alk. paper)
Subjects: LCSH: Technological innovations—Economic aspects—United States. |
   Inequality—United States.
Classification: LCC HC110.T4 G36 2019 | DDC 338/.0640973--dc23
LC record available at https://lccn.loc.gov/2019005650

10 9 8 7 6 5 4 3 2 1

Contents

Foreword

Lawrence H. Summers

The Industrial Revolution is rightly regarded as a major watershed in the history of humanity. After thousands of years when economic change was so slow as not to be noticeable within a single human life span, and where periods of regress were about as likely as periods of progress, all of a sudden enduring progress became the expectation.

Average living standards, which on the most generous of estimates rose by 50 percent from the time of Pericles in Athens to 1800 in London, started rising by 1 percent a year or even a bit more. Everything changed from the role of cities, to the nature of international relations, to relations between the genders, to demands on government, to the organization of business, to the meaning of property.

Taking a long enough view, the Industrial Revolution was a wonderful thing. People today live longer, more comfortably, and more fulfilling lives than they did two centuries ago. From child labor to surgery without anesthesia to slavery practices that were once seen as normal, today are seen in the industrial world as unthinkably barbaric.

But the long enough view speaks little to those whose wages fell when new spinning technologies were introduced and did not find new trades. It neglects the fact that the institutions we take for granted today, like government provided safety nets and universal education did not spring into being automatically, but resulted from a combination of moral necessity, aggressive and intelligent advocacy and political action. And it fails to reckon with the dramatic changes in the global order that took place in the wake of the industrial Revolution that culminated in arguably the two greatest manmade disasters in history—the two world wars.

I raise the Industrial Revolution because the book before us might be thought of as a kind of prehistory of the current and ongoing "Knowledge

Revolution," an event that I suspect historians in 2400 (if there still are historians in 2400) will see as being every bit as important as the Industrial Revolution. The Knowledge Revolution has likely been under way for several decades now as Information Technology has been transforming almost every aspect of economic life.

In some respects it has accelerated in the last decade. I often make this point to audiences by holding up my iPhone and observing: This $700 device has 1,000 times the computing power that put a man on the moon. It has more computing power than the most powerful computer on earth did when Bill Clinton was elected president. It provides more access to more knowledge than a Harvard University library card even though Harvard has one of the great libraries in the world. And it provides for more connectivity to more people more easily than the White House communications system could provide Lyndon B. Johnson with when he was the most powerful man on Earth. And very soon there will be more iPhones on Earth than there are adults.

The iPhone is about to be turbocharged by the addition of artificial intelligence. Speech recognition and facial recognition are not perfect, but they are on the verge of being better at these tasks than are humans. As I write this, it has just been demonstrated that AI can do a better job diagnosing eye disease from pictures than the best ophthalmologists. Already machines have produced poems, prints, and pieces of music that sophisticates cannot distinguish from those produced by real artists.

As with the Industrial Revolution, there is staggering potential for good in the Knowledge Revolution. But there will surely be large human costs along the way and there will be unexpected side effects that may have dire political consequences. It is the task of scholars and policy makers to maximize the benefits and minimize the adverse impacts.

This requires, as economists like me tend to emphasize, recognizing trade-offs and seeing them clearly. Probably more important, as the best political leaders always intuit and as the authors of this important book highlight, is to identify ways of cutting across trade-offs. This means finding ways of increasing efficiency and equity, of promoting both innovation for the society and security for the individual, of accelerating change while at the same time promoting enduring values.

In uncharted territory of this kind, there are two kinds of people—those who do not know they do not know, and those who do know they do not know. It is a great virtue of the present volume that its authors are squarely in the second camp. This leads them to present state of the art thinking on both sides of all the important questions, and to suggest policy approaches that are robust and so will work out well even when their premises turn out to have been off.

I concur with the sentiment often misattributed to Winston Churchill: the United States always does the right thing, but only after exhausting the alternatives. We are moving through many alternatives to the right thing at present. It is a scary time for us and for the world.

But we as a nation will come back just as we did when the Depression caused us to doubt the viability of capitalism, just as we did when Sputnik caused us to believe we would fall behind the Russians, just as we did when President Carter declared a crisis of the national spirit, just as we did when there was near universal agreement that "the Cold War was over and Japan has won."

The wisdom in this book about the shape of the world we are entering and about how we can shape that world is profound. The more it is absorbed the sooner will come the day when our adjustment to the Knowledge Revolution will be seen as yet another demonstration of our country's capacity for self-denying prophecies of doom.

Acknowledgments

Our thanks to Kevin Bryan, James Cham, Danny Gilligan, Nick Green, Richard Holden, Stephen King, Astrid Mastroni, Alex Tabarrok, and three anonymous referees for valuable comments on earlier drafts. At the MIT Press, Emily Taber provided superb editorial feedback.

Andrew dedicates this book to his wife Gweneth and our three innovative boys—Sebastian, Theodore, and Zachary—and the late Tony Atkinson, who devoted his career to the challenge of reducing inequality. Joshua dedicates this book to his recently departed advisers and inspirations: Ken Arrow, Nate Rosenberg, and Suzanne Scotchmer.

1   The Price of Progress

The United States today is more unequal than it has been in generations and more technologically advanced than ever. As the top 1 percent increases its share of the world's wealth, advances in artificial intelligence are driving new breakthroughs in facial recognition, language translation, and abstract strategy games. While the earnings gap between highly educated workers and the unskilled widens, CRISPR technology lets scientists edit genomes.

For robot designers, data analysts, and medical researchers, it can be the best of times. To paraphrase technology entrepreneur Jerry Kaplan, theirs is a future represented by *Star Trek*—a world where technology's benefits are widely shared.[1] For someone with few skills, few assets, and no job, it can feel like the worst of times. Theirs is a future that can seem like the dystopian one of *Terminator*, after a self-aware artificial intelligence realizes that it no longer needs humanity.

Some people argue that inequality is the price we must pay for innovation. They say that we can't all be billionaires. They assert that if we try to make society more equal by raising the top tax rate, it could deter risk taking and innovation. If we have to choose between having more stuff and distributing it fairly, they conclude that we should go for growth over equity.

We believe this is a false trade-off. Perhaps we can't all be billionaires, but there's no reason to be sanguine about rising inequality and falling mobility. The central argument of our book is that there are many ways that society can improve innovation and equality. This means we can have a bigger cake *and* slice it up more fairly. Indeed, when we overlook these ideas, we miss the chance to make society more entrepreneurial and more egalitarian.

Uneven Benefits

Over the past generation, all kinds of gaps have opened up in the labor market. Half a century ago, a high school graduate had to work for 1½ hours to earn what a college graduate earned in an hour. Now, a high school graduate must work for 2 hours to earn what a college graduate earns in an hour.[2] The wage gap between occupations has grown wider too. One study found that over the past quarter century, the wage increases received by janitors and security guards have been only one-tenth of the average for all employees.[3]

While the bottom is dropping out, the top is accelerating away. In today's dollars, CEOs of large firms in the mid-1960s earned, on average, around $900,000—a total that includes salary, bonuses, stock options, and incentive pay.[4] They currently earn $18.9 million. Put another way, the average worker back then would have had to work for 20 years to earn what their CEO took home in a year. Now, they would have to work for an impossible 312 years to earn the boss's annual salary.

Some people have dropped out of work altogether. Labor economists refer to people aged twenty-five to fifty-four as "prime aged." In the 1960s, the employment rate for men in this group was 94 percent. Since 2010, it has averaged just 83 percent.[5] Even prime-aged women, whose workforce participation rates skyrocketed in the postwar era, have a lower employment rate this decade than in the 1990s or 2000s.[6]

The US economy simply isn't delivering for many people. After inflation, median household income is only just above where it was in 1999.[7] Full-time wages for men are below where they were in 1973.[8] Since 1989, a household at the tenth percentile is barely better off, while a household at the ninetieth percentile has almost one-third more income.[9] The poverty rate, which fluctuates with the business and political cycle, is now where it was in 1969.[10] The child poverty rate is where it was in 1966.[11]

Let's put it another way. In the aggregate, men working full time haven't gotten a real pay raise since *American Graffiti* came out, and the typical household has about the same real income as it did when *The Matrix* was revealed. The child poverty rate is as bad now as when the Beatles toured. After inflation, households in the bottom tenth barely have more income than in the year Madonna released "Like a Prayer."

Admittedly, we need to be careful about what we're measuring. Compared to a generation ago, US employees are more likely to receive supplements to salaries, such as health care, private pension contributions, and on-site day care.[12] But these kinds of benefits only exacerbate inequality. Three-quarters of high earners have employer-provided health insurance, compared to just one-quarter of low earners.[13] Benefits such as free meals, paid volunteering days, and annual bonuses are more common in well-remunerated industries.

What's happening is divergence, big time.[14] From 1980 to 2014, the bottom half of US households saw their real incomes, after taxes and transfers, rise by only 0.6 percent each year. But for those at the top, it's a different story. Incomes for the top 10 percent have risen by 2 percent a year, while incomes for the top 1 percent have risen by 3 percent a year. At the very top, incomes for the top 0.001 percent have risen by 6 percent annually. In the mid-1990s, there were only about 100 billionaires worldwide. Now, there are 2,158. And that increase is not all the result of sweat and tears. In 2017, 44 people received an inheritance of more than $1 billion.[15]

Different Worlds

Having large sections of the population fall behind isn't inevitable. In the postwar decades, macroeconomic growth was strong, and equally distributed. In fact, from 1946 to 1980, incomes for the bottom half of the US population grew faster than incomes for the top half. But this came to an end in the 1980s.

In the postwar decades, regular Americans felt rich when they journeyed to Europe. Back in the early 1960s, the bottom half of US households were considerably richer—with incomes almost twice as high—than the bottom half of French households.[16] This position has been reversed. Now, the bottom half of Americans are about one-fifth poorer than the bottom half of French adults. From *Roman Holiday* to *An American in Paris*, classic movies used to feature Americans of modest means traveling to Europe. Low-income Americans simply can't afford Paris anymore.

One recent study looked at the issue by asking the simple question: What are the odds that a child earns a higher income than their parents?[17] For a child born in 1940, there was a 92 percent chance that they would end up living in a household with a higher income than the one they grew up in. But for a child born in 1980, this chance had fallen to just 50 percent. About two-thirds of this is due to the rise in inequality, with just one-third attributable to the fall in the overall rate of economic growth.

Wealth in the United States is becoming concentrated into fewer and fewer hands. In the mid-1980s, the bottom 90 percent of households controlled four times as much wealth as the top 0.1 percent.[18] Today, the two groups have the same shares. This means that in a population of slightly over 300 million, the top 300,000 or so have as much wealth as the bottom 270 million. It's a case of the "haves" versus the "have yachts."

Conveniences made possible by technology are also changing the nature of jobs, and which jobs are done by people and which are done by machines. From Prime to Alexa, Amazon is constantly on the lookout for innovations that can entice you to shop with it rather than at a local store. Amazon's Part Finder lets you point your smartphone camera at a screw, bolt, or washer to figure out what to order online. McDonald's is replacing human cashiers with digital-ordering kiosks. Pizza Hut stores in Japan and Singapore use Pepper the robot to take orders. In some clothing stores, smart cameras can scan your body shape to identify your size. It won't be long before artificial intelligence can suggest accessories with more accuracy than a human staff member.

Car factories have more robots and fewer workers than ever before. Fully automated warehouses can replace packers with robots, saving space, energy (robots can work in the dark), and time.[19] A joke imagines a factory in the future staffed by a person and a dog. The person's job is to feed the dog. The dog's job is to bite the human if they try to touch the machines.

In this book, our focus is on how to maximize the upside and minimize the downside of technology. We're both unabashed geeks, with a love for new gadgets and gizmos. We're excited by the potential of genetic medicine, 3-D printing, and virtual reality to make our lives healthier, more interesting, and longer than ever before. Just as technologies of the past have improved our lives, so too can the innovations to come.

But we're also painfully aware of the risk that technology drives a wedge through our society. In a world where robots can do everything and wages fall to zero, the only thing that matters is who owns the assets. That's a scary prospect for the one in five people whose wealth is already approximately zero. Even in more moderate scenarios, it's likely that the earnings gap between university graduates and high school dropouts will continue

to widen. That should be worrying for every teenager today who's considering not finishing school.

Is There a Big Trade-off?

In his 1975 book *Equality and Efficiency: The Big Tradeoff*, economist Arthur
Okun suggested that policy makers often have to choose between fairness
and growth. Take Supplemental Security Income, which is paid to disabled
and low-income elderly people. The payment reduces inequality. But it is
mostly funded by taxes on employment, which can dampen the incentive
to work more hours. Total income goes down, and equality goes up. Paying
taxes to keep the elderly out of poverty is a trade-off that most people are
happy to support.

The big question is whether a growing gap between rich and poor is the
price of progress. If we want to generate technological advances and innovations that improve productivity, must we accept that there will be some
who end up with a larger share of those fruits? Is there a trade-off between
innovation and equality?

Many in business and government say that inequality is merely the price
that society pays to enter into a more exciting world.[20] They rationalize this
position by saying that the focus should not be on inequality per se—who
gets more than me?—but instead on progress—am I better off than I was
before? Innovations are seen as things that make everyone better off even
if the gains differ. Yet in reality, "no losers" innovations are rare. Electronic
supermarket checkout machines displace cashiers today just as steel mills
displaced blacksmiths a century ago. Even as they raise average well-being,
most inventions make some people worse off.

Economists are also concerned about incentives. Innovations do not
come for free. Someone must devote effort and resources to bring new ideas
to market. Not surprisingly, they will only do so if they expect to be paid
back. Adjusting for risk, some profit is due them. So when we look back,
we will get innovations, but we will also likely see inequality. The fruits of
progress are unequally shared.

Seen in this light, extremely high top tax rates might impair innovation. In the final two years of World War II, the United States had a top tax
rate of 94 percent on incomes over $200,000.[21] For every additional dollar
above that threshold, the taxpayer kept just six cents. In that environment,

some entrepreneurs might hesitate. Push all tax rates up to 100 percent—the approach favored under pure communism—and the link between risk and reward is broken entirely. The result, as societies from Mao Tse-tung's China to Fidel Castro's Cuba have shown, is more equality but less innovation. In the end, everyone is worse off.

The problem with many contemporary debates over innovation and equality is that these extreme positions—innovation benefits everyone versus equality hurts everyone—have come to dominate the discussion. But once we move away from the fringes, we find many policies that do not imply a trade-off. Once you examine the details of technological innovation and its impacts, there are a plethora of good policies that allow both more innovation and less inequality. Okun's trade-off is often a false choice.

In this book, we argue that good policies are those that respect two fundamental facts about the process of innovation: creative destruction and unresolvable uncertainty. Creative destruction means that technological change comes at a cost, and this cost should be shared by those who receive the benefits. Unresolvable uncertainty means that policies should not be overly rigid and sector specific. Instead, we should think in insurance terms: how do we stimulate innovation while providing a buffer for those who disproportionately bear innovation's costs? In other words, how do we make redistribution smart?

Creative Destruction

In a world of fixed resources, technology provides a way to produce more output with the same inputs—to get more stuff out of the stuff we have. The way we do that is through discovery, and then the deployment of those discoveries. New knowledge lets us boost crop yields from the same land and seed. New knowledge allows us to make our computers more powerful with the same energy. New knowledge tells people how to identify diseases more accurately.

The question is: who pays the price for this progress? With inequality at levels not seen since the Gilded Age, is it reasonable to let the gap keep growing? Does society have to make a choice between innovation and inequality, or is it possible to have both?

Austrian-born economist Joseph Schumpeter did not suffer from excessive modesty. At the end of his life, he told friends that he had set himself three life goals: to be the greatest lover in Vienna, the best horseman in Austria, and the world's top economist. He said that he had attained two of these goals—but wouldn't disclose which ones.

In 1942, as a professor at Harvard, Schumpeter published *Capitalism, Socialism, and Democracy*, which popularized the idea of "creative destruction." He argued that new innovations would appear (that is, the creation part), and these would then account for progress. But in their wake were failed firms, lost jobs, and even obsolete industries (the destruction part). From this perspective, the price of progress falls into two broad categories: the price paid to get creation and the price paid in terms of destruction.

The *creation price* arises when the wealth of society is allocated to those who were the drivers of progress and away from those who were not. The people who drive progress need an appropriate reward for their efforts. Whatever remains should be allocated to others.

The *destruction price* focuses on the costs that arise when innovations and new technologies are introduced into the economy. Critically, the people who feel the costs are frequently different than those who receive the benefits. The destruction price can be disproportionately borne by those who are already vulnerable and who do not enjoy the gains in creation.

This is why innovation and inequality are intertwined. If our system involves those who create being rewarded for their efforts, then we must ensure that some of those rewards come back toward those who are harmed by new innovations. Both prices must be financed out of the rewards.

Unresolvable Uncertainty

Innovation typically involves two stages: exploration and exploitation. Initially, you might have a new technology (such as artificial intelligence or the CRISPR gene-editing tool). There may be ten ideas of how to create innovations out of this new technology. You do not know which one to pick. This is like closing your eyes and reaching into a bag of apples, some of which have gone bad. You might pull out a crisp one (representing a good idea to work on) or a rotten one (representing a bad idea). If you find a good apple, you move on from exploration (pulling apples from the bag) to exploitation (sinking your teeth into that good prospect).

Suppose I told you that in your bag of ten apples, there is a fifty-fifty chance there are nine crisp apples and a fifty-fifty chance there is only one crisp apple out of the ten. If you then pull out an apple and it turns out to be rotten, you will actually learn something about your prospects. Specifically, it is more likely that it is a bag with few crisp apples. Put your hand in a second time and get another rotten one, and you are even more sure. The point here is that using exploration, you learn more about what you are dealing with.

Remember that there are two kinds of possible bags. The good bag has nine out of ten crisp apples. The bad bag has just one out of ten crisp apples. If you're hungry, then the first challenge is to figure out whether you're holding a good or bad bag.

Chicago economist Frank Knight famously distinguished between risk and uncertainty. Risk, he said, was what happens when you know the probabilities. That is, you know how many rotten apples are in your bag of ten. But uncertainty is when you don't know the precise odds. In that case, you have to figure out what the whole bag looks like. Is the probability that there are lots of crisp apples 10 or 90 percent?

In this example, apple eating will always be risky, but it need not be uncertain. Once you've eaten two crisp apples from a bag, you know you must be holding a good bag of apples rather than a bad one. Now you can start munching Granny Smiths more readily than you would do if you were holding a bad bag of apples. Once you decide you've got a good bag, you've sorted out the issue of uncertainty. Now you can get on with taking risks.

Every innovator works in the realm of risk. Not even the world's top science laboratories have a 100 percent success rate. Even the best labs produce some dud ideas. But they try to ensure they're eating good bags of apples. They'll never stop being risk takers, but over time they can reduce their uncertainty about the fundamental idea-generating process.

Innovators don't immediately discover the best application of their technologies. Watt's steam engine was initially thought to be of use for pumping water from mines. It turned out to be the engine of the transportation revolution. At the dawn of the television age, 20th Century Fox cinema executive Darryl Zanuck scoffed, "Television won't be able to hold on to any market it captures after the first six months. People will soon get tired of staring at a plywood box every night." Lawyers at Bell Labs failed to patent the laser because they saw no applications for it in telecommunications. It underpinned not only CDs and DVDs but also optic fiber, the backbone of the internet.[22]

For these reasons, we take as our starting point that there is uncertainty regarding future technological change and uncertainty regarding its impact—including where and whether that impact will be favorable, unfavorable, or both. Any policy response must be predicated on this uncertainty. For instance, it makes little sense to develop new educational programs based on the forecast of the future of particular professions. Instead, we should ask ourselves whether current and future education programs are embracing uncertainty, and playing a role in helping protect people against unfavorable outcomes.

This is a common theme. When there is unresolvable uncertainty, we often need to consider policies in terms of their insurance value with respect to that uncertainty rather than their value in a particular state of the world.

The Path to Policy Ideas

In this book, we build our case in steps for policy ideas that promote innovation and reduce inequality. The first step is to explore the uncertainty that surrounds technological change. In chapter 2, we argue that it is difficult to be optimistic or pessimistic about our prospects for new technological innovations. There is a case to be made either way, and there is no good reason to bet one way or another. In chapter 3, we take a similar approach to the consequences of technological change should it occur. Will it be good or bad for jobs, and which ones? Uncertainty means we cannot forecast this with any degree of accuracy. Therefore, any policy should be based on uncertainty. You wouldn't bet your house on who's going to win the Super Bowl, so why stake everything on one particular technological vision of the future?

We then turn to consider the relationship between innovation and inequality. In chapter 4, we ask whether innovation requires inequality in order to happen. We then flip the question in chapter 5 by examining whether inequality is a consequence of innovation. In each case, we argue against any fixed relationship, looking at both the logic behind their underlying contentions and evidence to the contrary.

This leads to our policy explorations in chapters 6 and 7. Uncertainty means that when it comes to encouraging innovation, what is going to drive more of it is to improve outcomes on things we know. Innovators often know their costs, but have little information regarding their prospects.

Thus, it makes sense to choose policies that reduce the costs to innovators now rather than hypothetically giving them a higher return later on. When it comes to inequality, uncertainty means that we should adopt the philosophy of distributing the gains from innovation, but insuring people against the consequences of bearing the costs of those innovations. This means preferring policies that give people flexibility in their job options over their lifetime, and avoid locking or trapping them into the status quo.

Recent work by economists Jonathan Morduch and Rachel Schneider finds that a central challenge for low-income households is the high level of financial unpredictability and instability.[23] Seasonal work, unexpected shift changes, and casual work leads to income fluctuations. On top of this, unpredictable expenses, limited savings, and inadequate financial products frequently put them in the red. A missed utility bill can lead to the electricity or water being cut off. Missed rent payments can lead to eviction. At the extreme, bankruptcy beckons. Asked to choose between "financial stability" or "moving up the income ladder," three out of four people opted for financial stability.

We're all familiar with the idea of insurance in our own lives. You probably bought your first insurance policy when you bought your first car. You didn't know if you were going to have an accident, but you did know that if you smashed into a Rolls-Royce, then you'd be paying it off for the rest of your life. So you bought an insurance policy just in case.

Likewise, if you own a house, you've probably insured it against being burned down. If you're the family breadwinner, you may have life insurance to protect your loved ones against the loss of your income. Any time you're up against a calamitous risk, it's worth buying a fairly priced insurance policy.

A central idea in this book is that in the face of uncertainty, government should provide insurance. Some aspects of this are familiar. Health and unemployment insurance guard against the risks of sickness and job loss. Military and counterterrorism spending are an insurance policy against violent attacks. But the concept of insurance can also be extended to other areas of life. From permissionless innovation to generalist education, the insurance approach can help ensure we have more innovation and more equality. This book will explore the "insurance policies" that society might take out, and how they might bring us closer to the exciting age imagined by *Star Trek* than the corrupted future threatened by *Terminator*.

2 Renaissance or Dark Age?

It wasn't surprising the video went viral. It showed something magical: a hand tilting a ketchup bottle to about a forty-five-degree angle with its contents just sliding out. In twenty seconds, the bottle was entirely empty. No more banging your almost-empty ketchup bottle to extract the final dollop.[1]

But ketchup was just one application for LiquiGlide, the MIT-originated start-up that had cracked the puzzle of liquid leftovers. The company's technology coated the insides of containers with a thin film that did not leave the bottle, but created a surface across which the bottle's contents would quickly travel. LiquiGlide is also applying its technology to other fluids, including agricultural chemicals and medications.

Large innovations are usually ones no one sees coming. The most significant consumer innovation of the last decade was announced on January 9, 2007. Despite uneven health, Apple CEO Steve Jobs took the stage at the Macworld Conference in San Francisco and unveiled the iPhone. Ten years later, one billion iPhones had been sold. Today, many think touch screen smartphones are as necessary as underwear and more important than socks.

Yet when Jobs launched his revolutionary phone, many believed it would fail. Microsoft's CEO, Steve Ballmer, laughed at the device, calling it a "not very good email machine." At the time, BlackBerry, a smartphone with a smaller screen and mini keyboard, controlled half the smartphone market.[2] People loved their BlackBerries so much that they were called CrackBerries. One of the reasons Hillary Clinton kept her private email server (which probably cost her the presidency) was so she could keep using her Black-Berry. When the iPhone appeared, BlackBerry's inventor, Mike Lazaridis, dismissed its core design: "Try typing a web key on a touch screen on an Apple iPhone; that's a real challenge. You cannot see what you type." Black-Berry's market capitalization has since fallen by nine-tenths.

These people were all wrong, and wrong in a major way. As industry insiders, they all paid the price for their poor predictions. The old companies would all exit the industry replaced by the new Apple, of course, but also Samsung and Huawei. The point is not to turn the laughter back on the disrupted but instead to note that even what turns out to be a successful innovation might not seem that way at first. There is a reason for that: innovation is new to the world. If it was obvious, someone would have done it.

Technology forecasts can also be wrong in the other direction. In 2001, after years of stealth development, inventor Dean Kamen unveiled the Segway. This was a personal transporter, constructed with two wheels on either side of a platform with a stick and handlebar jutting from its center. At a time when computer-controlled gyroscopes were rare, it seemed like magic. Implausibly, the Segway would balance itself and its occupant upright. The rider simply leaned forward to accelerate and backward to stop. The Segway seemed like something from the future. It seemed like something that you wanted to try.

To many others, the Segway was heralded as a revolution. Jobs said it was "as big a deal as the PC." John Dorr, the famous venture capitalist behind Netscape and Amazon, believed it would be bigger than the internet.[3] Apart from concerns about the price (Segways initially sold for $3,000), it is hard to find many early detractors. Alas, a decade and a half later, you might see a Segway used by a traffic cop or group of tourists being led around a city. Otherwise, it is a discarded technological concept.

Why didn't the Segway work out? It wasn't because it didn't work. It did. There were some safety issues, but that hasn't prevented the police from adopting them. One theory is that people stuck out too much on them, drawing attention in an unwelcome way. The point is that our forecasts—optimistic or pessimistic—for individual technologies can often be way off base. Marc Andreessen, Netscape founder and venture capitalist, compares his performance with that of Warren Buffett, the world-famous proponent of "value investing": "Basically, he's betting against change. We're betting for change. When he makes a mistake, it's because something changes that he didn't expect. When we make a mistake, it's because something doesn't change that we thought would."[4]

We start this discussion of technological prospects with the iPhone and Segway precisely because of this question of far-reaching impact. The iPhone established a dominant design for smartphones. Thanks to people having the internet in their pocket, we got Uber, Airbnb, and Spotify. We got Facebook, Instagram, LinkedIn, and Twitter to inform, engage, and infuriate us. Developing economies skipped over bank accounts to mobile banking, such as Kenya's ubiquitous M-Pesa service. If the doubters had been right, we would have had none of these things. For the Segway, we didn't end up changing urban transportation. Billions might have switched to a travel technology that eased congestion and cut emissions. We didn't. Instead of transforming cities, those environments are just where we left them.

Before considering the impact of new innovations on inequality, we have to ask whether there are still big breakthroughs to be made. As we will demonstrate in this chapter, economists disagree. There are technological optimists who believe that big breakthrough innovations lie in our future, and pessimists who believe they won't surpass the past. How can we evaluate their arguments?

The Tech Optimists

In early 2014, owners of Tesla's Model S electric vehicles received a recall notice from the US National Highway Traffic Safety Administration about a problem that could cause a fire. What car owners usually had to do in that instance was return the car to a dealer so that fixes could be put in place. This was costly for everyone involved. This time, however, it was different: Tesla identified the issue as one that could be fixed by updating the software in the car. Because Teslas are connected by default to the internet, the update could be pushed to almost thirty thousand vehicles overnight. No muss, no fuss.

But it is not just the convenience of dealing with safety concerns that Tesla owners enjoy from all this. The company regularly pushes out updates that enhance the capabilities of the cars. As Hurricane Irma approached Florida, Tesla pushed out a software upgrade that gave drivers an additional forty miles of range.[5] Moreover, every Tesla that leaves the factory has the hardware necessary for full self-driving capabilities. Over the coming years, the firm will be able to steadily upgrade the software in the cars so that the vehicles can become self-driving.

The power of software to enhance hardware is nothing new. Two Voyager space probes left Earth in the 1970s for a tour of the solar system. By the time they reached the outer solar system in the late 1980s, their systems had been upgraded to allow for better-quality images as well as better compression for them. In other words, the pictures being taken were better than when the probes were launched. The fact that this can be achieved for so many things today that have embedded software in them caused Andreessen to proclaim that "software was eating the world."[6] Put simply, real things were no longer fixed in their capabilities. Because of software, they could be enhanced without having to physically rebuild them.

New York University's Paul Romer, a recent Nobel laureate, is the founder of the "new growth theory." Romer likens the discovery of new ideas to blending chemical elements. Past inventors combined tin and copper to get bronze, and mixed carbon with iron to produce steel. But that's just the start.

> To get some sense of how much scope there is for more such discoveries, we can calculate as follows. The periodic table contains about a hundred different types of atoms. If a recipe is simply an indication of whether an element is included or not, there will be 100×99 recipes like the one for bronze or steel that involve only two elements. For recipes that can have four elements, there are $100 \times 99 \times 98 \times 97$ recipes, which is more than 94 million. With up to 5 elements, more than 9 billion. Mathematicians call this increase in the number of combinations "combinatorial explosion."
>
> Once you get to 10 elements, there are more recipes than seconds since the big bang created the universe. As you keep going, it becomes obvious that there have been too few people on earth and too little time since we showed up, for us to have tried more than a minuscule fraction of all the possibilities.[7]

Romer's point is that the number of ideas that we are yet to explore and turn into useful knowledge is potentially limitless—at least in terms of our own time horizon. In other words, if people are expecting technological change, a simple examination of what is physically possible isn't going to dash those expectations.

The tech optimists are not optimistic simply because they know that the universe has more to reveal. They are optimistic because they believe that we are still living in a time of accelerating technological change. Andreessen argues that the benefits of computing technologies and the digitization revolution are ongoing because they are based on software—something that scales easily.

More than half the world's population came online in just the past decade, and the world is not yet fully connected. Moreover, the value of that network increases disproportionately to the number of people on it. This is an effect known as Metcalfe's law. Imagine you were thinking about what happens as people adopt more communications technology, such as a messaging platform like WhatsApp or WeChat. If two people join the platform, then one linkage is possible between them. If another person then joins, there are three possible connections. Even without a group chat option, the increase in connections by adding one person is greater. Add another person and you have six possible pairwise connections. So the value of the network rises exponentially as you add more people.

From the perspective of an innovator in software, that means its customer base is still growing rapidly. What is more, with greater numbers of users, distributed infrastructure—known commonly as "the cloud"—becomes cheaper to utilize even aside from the reductions in the cost of hardware in data centers. In 2000, it may have cost a start-up $150,000 per month to host an internet application in the cloud. Today it is less than $150. Those gains translate into increased profitability and lower risk for every single software entrepreneur.

The savviest companies now bet on change occurring. In 2004, Google launched its Gmail web-based email service to the public. When it did so, it offered 1 GB of free storage space. This stunned the market. The main service at the time, Hotmail, offered 2 MB (500 times less). Google's announcement was made on April 1, so people thought it was just one of the company's famous April Fools' Day pranks. It wasn't. The firm had observed that the cost of storage was falling and would continue to drop. Google didn't go so far as to offer unlimited storage, but it told its customers to stop worrying about deleting emails and instead keep everything. This was a shock to an industry where email providers had often profited by selling additional storage to people who did not want to delete precious emails. That business model died on April 1, 2004. An optimistic bet paid off for Google, and today Gmail has over a billion active users worldwide.

Tech optimists point to multiple trends. Since the 1960s, Moore's law saw processing power double roughly every eighteen to twenty-four months. This trend was first noticed by Intel's Gordon Moore. Initially, gains came from increasing the density of transistors on chips. More recently, improvements have still come from adding more cores, building systems on a chip, and improving the yields in the production of chips so that costs come down. As a consequence, microprocessors in 2018 had 8 million times as many transistors as the best microprocessor in 1971.[8] Worldwide data storage is now around a zettabyte, or 10^{21} bytes. Each minute, three hundred hours of video are uploaded to YouTube. The next mobile telephony standard, 5G, will operate at multiple times the speed of the previous generation of wireless technology.

Technologies are sometimes used in unexpected ways. Graphics processing units (developed for hard-core gamers) were used to train neural networks designed to emulate the learning functions of the brain. These new developments in what is called machine learning have led to a renaissance in artificial intelligence research. Erik Brynjolfsson and Andrew McAfee have termed this the "second machine age."[9] The first machine age accompanied the steam engine and Industrial Revolution that allowed physical strength to be surpassed. This one would be all about mental strength. Its proponents view it as equally transformative.

Around five years ago, using deep learning methods pioneered by several Canadian university professors, the ability of computers to understand speech and recognize images took a leap forward.[10] These new methods mimicked the brain function, and allowed multiple levels of sorting and classification. The result was effectively allowing computers to pick up nuance and associations that even humans would miss. Machines are now better than people at recognizing faces. Facial recognition algorithms used by Baidu, Tencent-BestImage, Google, and DeepID3 now have an accuracy level above 99.5 percent.[11] By contrast, humans have an accuracy rate of 97.6 percent.[12] In October 2016, Microsoft engineers announced that their speech recognition software had attained the same level of accuracy as human transcribers when it came to recognizing speech in the "Switchboard Corpus," a set of conversations used to benchmark transcribers.[13] In a controlled environment, machine voice recognition is now more likely to comprehend what we're saying than the average human.

One way to mark the progress of artificial intelligence is in playing the world's toughest games. In 1997, machines overtook humans in chess, when IBM's Deep Blue beat world champion Garry Kasparov. Two decades later, the contest turned to Go, an ancient Chinese game with many more possible moves and strategies than chess. In 2016, Google's AlphaGo beat Lee Sedol, one of the world's best players. The following year, it trounced the world champion, Ke Jie. The performance gap between AlphaGo and Ke is now about as large as the gap between Ke and a keen amateur.[14] AlphaGo is not just unbeatable by humans; it performs at an entirely new level. If the world's best chess and Go computers were self-aware, they might look at our prowess in their games the way that we regard the intellectual powers of our pets.

The best way to explain what has happened is to focus in on what the new artificial intelligence techniques do best: prediction.[15] Machines can now take a large amount of data (numbers, images, sound files, or videos) and review it for relationships that allow them to forecast with a high degree of accuracy. Image recognition, for example, is basically a prediction activity: "Here is a picture. What is your best guess at what someone would call this?"

Although these technologies still make mistakes, they have the ability to outperform humans in real-world contexts. In 2011, IBM's Watson computer played the quiz show *Jeopardy!* against two champions of the game: Ken Jennings and Brad Rutter. Watson won. IBM's next major human versus machine contest came in 2018, when the company showed off its "IBM Debater." The computer was able to engage at a reasonably coherent level with a human counterpart on the topic of whether government should subsidize space exploration.[16]

Such machines are still well away from passing the Turing test, in which a computer can fool people into thinking they are dealing with a fellow human being. But they are steadily getting better. One possible breakthrough may come from attempts to build artificial intelligence machines that can themselves build artificial intelligence machines—a research project that Google has dubbed "AutoML."[17] Over recent years, there has been a steady flow of artificial intelligence experts from universities to work with firms such as Google (Geoff Hinton), DeepMind (Rich Sutton), Facebook (Yann LeCun), Apple (Ruslan Salakhutdinov), Uber (Raquel Urtasun), Baidu (Andrew Ng), and Microsoft (Yoshua Benigio). AutoML has also created concerns that the technology could become unstoppable—an issue we will return to below.

Learning machines do not have to just rely on their own experience. They can treat the experience of other machines as their own and then all learn together.

It does not take much to imagine what other things machines could pick up with a little time and a lot of experience. Identifying lung nodules on a patient's scan: check. Drafting a legal contract, based on earlier examples: check. Choosing the best calculus problem to teach a struggling student:

check. Scheduling an appointment: check. If it can be described, it can be learned.

Indian online retailer Myntra recently deployed an algorithm that designed new clothing images by modifying and combining popular patterns.[18] One of those computer-designed T-shirts, featuring blocks of olive, blue, and yellow, is now a best seller. Artificial intelligence is arguably the next general-purpose technology. These are the technologies that are so foundational that a myriad of other innovations grows on their base. We have seen this happen with the steam engine, electric power, plastics, computers, and the internet. The optimists believe that artificial intelligence could have the same potential.[19]

To see how technology might drive science, remember that Galileo's research—which showed convincingly that the earth revolved around the sun—was based on a technological advance in the form of a telescope that could magnify distant objects thirty times. A few decades later, the creation of a microscope that could magnify tiny things three hundred times enabled Robert Hooke to document the existence of cells. These massive breakthroughs in astronomy and biology would have been impossible without technological advances in glass production and precision manufacturing.

Today, it's easy to point to similar advances. The use of gene editing could revolutionize medical science. Strong and light materials such as graphene could change manufacturing. These are radical technologies that could bring about decades of further innovation.

The Tech Pessimists

The tech pessimists take an altogether dimmer view of our future prospects. They worry that we have already picked the low-hanging fruit in the last two centuries, and that the outlook for the next century is more barren. Their argument is not based on some oracle-like insight into the future but instead on the inescapable economic law of diminishing returns.

In economics, the figure that looms largest in terms of a tech pessimist viewpoint is Robert Gordon. The core of his concern revolves around just how great the relatively recent past has been. Prior to 1870, economic growth occurred at a trickle. But after 1870, the major innovations at the heart of the Industrial Revolution began to work their way fully through society. It wasn't just that steam power made factories more efficient; our knowledge of science also brought us to a point where new technologies were shaping the environment around us.

In the century following 1870, most people in the United States and western Europe (and a handful of other places) went from carrying water to having it delivered to their houses at the turn of a tap, instantly and in a form safe enough to drink. Washing machines saved time and made our clothes last longer. Indoor toilets took sewage far away from houses at the push of a lever or yank of a chain. Energy could be easily delivered to people's houses. Information was brought in by the radio, telephone, and television. Cars provided freedom and reshaped the urban form. A reasonable person might suppose that society will never again see such radical changes.[20] The interesting thing is that we can see this in our data on economic growth that measures how innovations have translated into productivity improvements. And the trouble appeared in 1973—the year the party ended.

Growth has its ups and downs. But smooth out the temporary recessions and upswings, and the century until 1973 was an era of steady progress that suddenly petered out. Initially, many economists saw the slowdown as an aberration. Nobel laureate Bob Solow, who pioneered the field of economic growth, said in 1987 that "you can see the computer age everywhere but in the productivity statistics."[21] Maybe it was a mismeasurement because computers were assisting services, whose productivity was notoriously hard to measure? The economic historian Paul David reminded people that when electricity was introduced, it took decades for it to show up in measures of productivity. Maybe once firms worked out how to use computers effectively, the productivity gains would become apparent?[22]

In the late 1990s, many advanced nations did experience a surge in productivity growth. Yet the rate of productivity growth then slowed in the twenty-first century. For workers, things are even worse because of a decoupling of wages from productivity. Even where firms are getting more output for a given level of inputs, they are not sharing most of those gains with employees.

Consequently, there is a generation of adults who have not experienced the fruits of productivity improvements. They are as well educated as their immediate forebears, they are more lightly taxed, and the businesses that employ them have the benefits of more integrated global financial markets. On paper (or perhaps we should say on screen), there is no apparent reason why the four decades after 1973 should not have been as fruitful as the three decades following World War II. But a considered analysis away from the commercial and political hype tells us otherwise.

The problem comes down to something economists call "diminishing returns." In the nineteenth century, David Ricardo noted that as England continued to put more land under farming, the productivity of additional acres was going down. Take any fixed resource and there is only so much you can extract from it. In the twentieth century, Solow observed that this held for other types of capital such as machines. It also applied to workers.

Prior to Solow, economists heavily emphasized the value of saving. Capital makes labor more productive, many economists argued, that people should sacrifice consumption today to invest and build capital that will give them even more tomorrow. Growth was intertwined with savings. This appealed to both the Right (which saw it as a recognition of the value of personal thrift) and Left (which regarded it as an affirmation of the value of governments using tax revenue to invest). Either way, the theory predicted that in an economy that didn't draw on other countries' savings, a higher savings rate would boost economic growth.

Along with Australian economist Trevor Swan, Solow dashed that notion. Sure, they said, if you push the savings rate from 10 to 20 percent, you will get a spurt in growth. More capital will be created per unit of labor, and with that expansion in resources, output will rise. But that capital must be combined with labor and made from scarce materials. That means that even if you could invest so that you could generate $1,000 per person more in income this year, the same investment is unlikely to get you the same improvement in future years as the law of diminishing returns kicks in. Income per person may well end up higher than before, but the growth rate itself will fall back to where it was.

While this sunk the idea that simply increasing the rate of savings could set sustained improvements in income per capita in perpetual motion, the puzzle remained that people were steadily getting richer. Why might this be occurring? The answer was that since the Industrial Revolution, there had been sustained technical progress (literally, improvements in how much we can draw from fixed resources). Whether it be by learning, the applications of science, or more open institutions for experimentation and entrepreneurship, new ideas were being created and put into practice. Those things could get you sustained growth without having to adjust anyone's savings habits.

We arrive at the crux of the matter. So long as the growth in knowledge we had achieved in the past continued into the future, there was nothing to be worried about. Yet here is where the tech optimists and tech pessimists part company. The optimists, as we have noted, anticipate rapid technological progress. The pessimists are not so sure. If that is the case, they say, then what happened after 1973? Why have this generation's inventions not transformed our lives in the way of the great twentieth-century innovations? Do the twenty-first century's inventions really compare with air-conditioning, airplanes, and automobiles (to take just one letter of the alphabet)?

To tech pessimists such as Gordon and Tyler Cowen, the answer comes from merely looking at how technological changes from the 1870s to the 1970s transformed the way we live. Electricity transformed work, shifting people from agriculture to the cities. In the cities that combined with running water, sewerage systems, and efficient heating and cooling systems: allowing for a comfortable and productive urban life. Electrical appliances reshaped household economics, freeing women to join the paid labor force. Transport on the roads and air was transformed, facilitating an unprecedented interregional trade and travel. All this added up to dramatic improvements in productivity. Since 1973, there have been useful inventions to be sure. But they are yet to deliver an equivalent surge in productivity.

What has the pessimists worried is that researchers and scientists are finding it harder to unearth new ideas. Research by Northwestern's Ben Jones shows that Nobel laureates are getting older. To be more precise, over the past century the age someone does research that will win them a Nobel Prize has been rising. The same is true of work that leads to a patent. In addition, more knowledge breakthroughs are being done by teams rather than individuals. This points to more specialization in knowledge production with fewer instances in which an individual comprehends developments at the frontier of multiple disciplines. Jones calls this the increasing "burden of knowledge" since it raises the cost of innovating.[23]

As technology advances, it becomes tougher to find the next new thing. Take semiconductors. As we have noted, Moore's law has seen a steady doubling of the density of computer chips every eighteen to twenty-four months. Moore's law continued up until the mid-2000s, but significantly, the *cost* of recent increases is eighteen times larger than what it costs for similar proportionate increases in the 1970s.[24] The same pattern exists in agriculture and medical research. What was once easy has become hard. It suggests that just to keep the slower growth in productivity that we have, innovators must run faster and faster.

Uncertain Prospects

Between the tech optimists and tech pessimists, it is easy to see that both have a point. The optimists note that there is still potential for new knowledge, and can point to potentially exciting developments that are attracting significant scientific and engineering resources. The pessimists' colder calculations remind us how exceptional past growth was and the logical implication that those ideas that gave the biggest boosts to productivity were likely ones that have already been exploited. Historians such as Joel Mokyr have looked at all this discussion and remind us that we have been here before. In every decade, one can find optimists and pessimists, and at least as far as continuing technological change is concerned, the optimists have usually been on the right side of history.[25]

What does this all mean, however, for the creation price—that is, the price that must be paid to reward innovators and entrepreneurs for their efforts? The answer lies in the cost of innovation. Where the tech optimists and tech pessimists fundamentally differ is about how costly it will be to innovate in the future. If there are technological opportunities just waiting to be exploited, as the optimists claim, then the creation price can be set relatively low. On the other hand, if the cost of innovation is rising, as the pessimists claim, then the creation price will be higher, and growing over time. More resources will have to be dedicated to innovative activities to maintain historic growth rates. In that situation, we will have to ask if it is a price with paying.

Forecasting the future is like driving through fog. We need to accept that the level of the creation price is uncertain. It could be high, low, or somewhere in between. It will likely be different for different technological opportunities and directions. But at the same time, everyone faces this uncertainty. No one has a special insight into the future. That includes entrepreneurs. And given that uncertainty, the best way to get more equality and more innovation is to reduce the costs those entrepreneurs face today.

3 Superpowers or Annihilation?

It was 1589, and in a small village near Nottingham in England, William Lee invented a machine that could knit stockings. His stocking frame is one of the earliest examples of mechanization in textiles some two centuries before the Industrial Revolution. Stockings were much sought after in the Middle Ages, but Lee's invention was not universally celebrated. Indeed, when he was finally able to present his invention to Queen Elizabeth I (known to be partial to knitted silk stockings), she refused to grant him a patent. Why? The queen feared it would put many hand knitters out of work.[1]

This story is not unusual. Something is invented that has the potential to give ordinary people something akin to superpowers. But society resists it because of fear of the social impacts. Unlike other negative consequences that might arise from new innovations—and we are thinking here primarily of environmental pollution—what is instructive about inventions such as Lee's is that they are resisted not because of their unintended effects but instead because of their intended ones.

Lee himself, according to some accounts, was not entirely innocent in this regard. He was said to have been enamored of a young woman in the village who paid him no attention. She happened to be a knitter and teacher of knitters, and Lee felt that her attention was there rather than toward him. This caused him to pour his energies in trying to remove any need for anyone—this woman included—to knit by hand. Three years later, he had built a machine that could take the job of the woman who had spurned him.

After being denied a patent by the queen, Lee was unable to find patronage to develop a mechanized business in England and went to France. While he was more welcome there, things did not end well, and he eventually died in poverty. Lee's brother ended up bringing the frame back to Nottingham.

It took over two centuries for mechanized knitting to be adopted by factory owners, but when it was, the backlash from workers came quickly.

In 1811, disgruntled textile workers wrote to factory owners under the pen name Ned Ludd, threatening to smash machines if they continued to be used. Across northern England, thousands of Luddites joined together to burn factories and break up knitting frames. As the legend grew, Ludd was supposed to live in Sherwood Forrest, like Robin Hood. So seriously did the British government take the Luddite rebellion that breaking textile machines was made a capital offense. Before the movement was quashed in 1816, there were more British soldiers fighting the Luddites than battling Napoléon I. Yet the Luddites' fear of overall job loss was ill founded. In the decade from 1811 to 1821, the British economy added over three hundred thousand jobs—an increase of more than 10 percent.[2]

Concern about the impact of innovation on jobs is almost as old as inventions themselves. In the first century AD, Roman emperor Tiberius was said to have murdered the inventor of "unbreakable glass" in order to ensure that the new creation didn't put glassmakers out of work.[3] In 1930, British economist John Maynard Keynes warned of "technological unemployment," worrying that "the increase of technical efficiency has been taking place faster than we can deal with the problem of labor absorption." In 1964, a group of Nobel prizewinners warned US president Lyndon Baines Johnson of a revolution triggered by "the combination of the computer and the automated self-regulating machine."[4] In 1983, Russian-American economist Wassily Leontief forecast that "labor will become less and less important. More and more workers will be replaced by machines. I do not see that new industries can employ everybody who wants a job."[5] Since then, the US economy has added more than fifty million jobs.

Sometimes history has been quick to rebut the doomsayers. In 1940, US president Franklin Delano Roosevelt told Congress that double-digit unemployment had created "an army of unused youth," posing a challenge for the economy to "[find] jobs faster than invention can take them away."[6] But by the end of the decade, the United States was enjoying full employment, at least for men. The mass production of munitions during wartime, followed by a postwar surge in house building and the manufacture of consumer goods, ensured enough jobs for virtually every man who wanted one.

In the previous chapter, we discussed those who are optimistic and pessimistic about prospects for future innovation. Here, we look at the divergence of views about what it means for jobs. Will future technology cause mass unemployment, or will the labor market adapt, as it did in the era of the Luddites, Keynes, and Leontief?

The more optimistic you are about the pace of technological change, the more urgent it becomes to think about the labor market. But tech pessimists still worry about net job destruction. Even if advances in technology are slower today than in previous eras, the capability of machines to replicate human talents raises the risk that some workers will be left unemployable.

As consumers, we often buy new gadgets because they save us time. Similarly, employers frequently buy machines because they will save their workforce time. This raises concerns over whether companies will use automation as a means of shedding workers. If the machines are adopted across the economy, will there be enough jobs for all?

On the topic of optimism and pessimism about technological progress, the tech pessimists tended to draw on evidence from history to argue that the pace of innovation is slowing down. Conversely, when we look at the impact on employment, the optimists are apt to ground their arguments in history. Those most worried about jobs in a technological age are generally the ones who contend that "this time it's different."

So again, we begin with the optimists, and see what they have to say about how today's new technologies might affect employment.

The Job Optimists

Let's start with the more mundane or, at least, less romanticized of jobs: bookkeeping. In 1985, there were two million bookkeepers in the United States. Today there are only about one million.[7] What happened to them? The spreadsheet.

In the late 1970s, Harvard MBA student Dan Bricklin was frustrated at the time it was taking to work through cases for his courses. The cases came with a list of financial figures. "Cracking the case" involved exploring that data and calculating what might happen if the managers made different choices. As a software engineer, Bricklin wrote a program that would allow you to input this data, calculate relevant statistical summaries and formula, and then change entries without having to recalculate everything by hand. It was a calculator on steroids.

The idea worked, and Bricklin teamed up with Bob Frankston to commercialize their software. The result was VisiCalc, which Steve Wozniak (the inventor of the Apple I and II computers) called the first killer app for personal computers. If you look at VisiCalc, it will be familiar to you. It has the same numbered rows and lettered columns as Microsoft Excel and Google Sheets. VisiCalc and other spreadsheet software replaced much of the day-to-day tasks of bookkeepers.[8]

While the world may lament the disappearance of local butchers and bakers, there are no songs for the bookkeepers. Not even those who lost out to the spreadsheet seem to lament their former craft. Why? Because the software opened up possibilities for people to become spreadsheet users. Employees who might once have worked as bookkeepers are now accountants and analysts. There are almost twice as many accountants and auditors (1.8 million now), and 2.1 million financial analysts. Of the million people who ceased working as bookkeepers, it is likely that many, freed from the most routine and boring parts of their job, moved into being spreadsheet masters rather than spreadsheet discards.

A similar story was documented in Margot Lee Shetterly's book *Hidden Figures* (which has been made into a hit film). This tracked the story of three African American women in the 1960s who worked in various highly skilled jobs at the National Aeronautics and Space Administration (NASA). One of them—Dorothy Vaughan—supervised a group of other African Americans called "computers." These women did the job—apparently beneath male engineers—of calculating the numerical results of complex mathematical formulas. In the movie, Vaughan is depicted seeing NASA installing a new IBM mainframe computer whose task was to do those computations that kept the women employed. She quickly realizes, however, that programming the mainframe was itself a skilled task that no one had yet mastered. She and her team understood what was involved in computation, so by learning to program, they were in the best position to take the new jobs. Vaughan ended up managing that unit and later the entire computing division.

It is stories like this that make some relaxed about employment prospects. Boston University's Jim Bessen has documented other reassuring historical examples.[9] Bank tellers weren't replaced by ATMs; they just stopped doing the "telling" of cash and instead started playing a role in what is now called "relationship banking." The average number of employees at each branch fell by a third, but banks decided to open up many more branches.

When desktop publishing software was introduced, Sears laid off one hundred people producing its famed catalog. But because desktop publishing lowered the cost of producing marketing documents, more companies started churning out catalogs, and employment in direct marketing grew. In each case, the job category most at risk ended up thriving.

What about driverless vehicles? Request an Uber in Pittsburgh, and in 2018, you might have found yourself stepping into an autonomous Ford Fusion. Fitted with twenty cameras and a rotating laser sensor on the roof, the cars move smoothly through the city—braking quickly when they spot pedestrians, obeying traffic signals, and sticking to the speed limit. One can imagine that for a child, being in such a self-driving car is no different from their ordinary experience. For adults, the wonder quickly turns to imagining what you might do with your time when you don't have to pay attention to the road.

According to a recent report from Goldman Sachs's economics research, around four million US workers work as drivers. Yet these drivers are not about to be unemployed tomorrow. Uber's Pittsburgh cars do not employ drivers. But they do have "safety drivers" whose job it is to sit in the driver's seat ready to take over if necessary. In Phoenix, Alphabet's Waymo say that it will soon remove the safety driver from its ride-hailing vehicles.[10] At the time of writing, this had not occurred. Net job loss so far: zero.

Naturally, Uber and Waymo would not be exploring the option of driverless cars if they did not think that they could remove the safety drivers at some point in the future. But change is likely to come more slowly than some predict. To date, most progress on autonomous vehicles has been made in highly controlled environments, such as amusement parks and airport rail shuttles. Some cities like Copenhagen have fully automated commuter trains, but progress in making autonomous vehicles work "off the rails" has been limited.

Progress by firms such as Waymo, Tesla, General Motors' Cruise Automation, and Intel's Mobileye has been made possible thanks to advances in neural networks. Neural networks are a previously dormant side of artificial intelligence that experienced a revival when complex environments were capable of being represented and captured in a machine-readable data form. Now such machines can take in information from the road, in real time, and form a picture of the road. What's more, it is dynamic. They can predict what other cars are likely to do and then act accordingly. Prediction matters because the choices you make when you drive a car are simple: stop, go, slow down, accelerate, and turn. You can explain to a child why you do those things. If you've ever taught a teenager to drive, though, you'll know that one of the tricks is to improve their ability to predict how the traffic around them is likely to behave.

There are many potential benefits of driverless cars. First, there is the safety angle. Right now, about a hundred people a day die in traffic accidents in the United States. This figure would not drop to zero with the advent of driverless cars, but we could expect a dramatic reduction. Like airplane disasters, the handful of deaths associated with driverless cars has garnered significant media attention, but every indication is that the technology will save lives.

The second main category of benefits is in time savings. Cars provide freedom, but also waste time. The typical driver spends fifty-one minutes a day in the car.[11] Driverless cars will induce more people to commute by car, but because of their greater efficiency, experts estimate that a road network dominated by driverless cars would have half as much congestion.[12] Meanwhile, the person who was formerly driving the car could be freed up to read, write, sleep, or watch movies. Self-driving vehicles could even specialize in offering services to commuters, such as a hairdresser or gym.[13] Similar technology could allow food stands and retail stores to come to you, returning in the middle of the night to restock at a central depot.

Nonetheless, there are significant limits on the uptake of driverless cars. One is handling bad weather. If you live in a snowy city, think about whether you perfectly obey the road rules after a snowstorm (e.g., you might drive more toward the center of the road to reduce the risk of sliding off the edge). At present, driverless cars' sensors do not work properly at dawn and dusk. They struggle to handle heavy rain.

Another challenge is driving in congested urban areas. In a city such as Boston, where traffic tends to follow norms rather than rules, a driverless vehicle might be stuck for hours at an intersection if it waits for a clean gap rather than being willing to push into busy traffic. Navigating a truck through narrow city streets is a task that takes drivers years to master. Similarly, we are not yet at a point where autonomous vehicles can handle a tricky situation such as a police officer waving traffic through a red light.[14]

Regulators will need to resolve some thorny ethical issues. Suppose you are the only person in a car driving along a cliffside road and four children recklessly run out. Should your autonomous vehicle swerve over the edge, sacrificing the life of one versus four? Or should the car take a rules-based approach, putting the life of the diligent driver above that of the jaywalking pedestrians? When MIT researchers put scenarios like these to millions of people around the world, most opted for utilitarianism—the outcome that achieves the greatest good for the greatest number.[15]

Specific scenarios like the cliffside driver will be rare, but they are relevant to programming the driving style of autonomous vehicles. As MIT study coauthor Iyad Rahwan observes, "If you stay relatively near to the cycle lane, you're increasing the chance of hitting a cyclist, but reducing the chance of hitting another car in the next lane over. Repeat that over hundreds of millions of trips, and you're going to see a skew in the [accident] statistics."[16] Setting clear ground rules will be essential to the uptake of driverless cars, since no manufacturer will want to be left open to lawsuits. Yet the MIT study found that people in different regions of the world varied in how much weight they would place on harm to the elderly, high-status individuals, or pets. It would be a major undertaking if these national differences were embodied in the software that governs self-driving cars (to say nothing about whether cars would need to be reprogrammed when they crossed borders). Before driverless cars can start taking the jobs of millions of drivers, the laws governing these issues need to be settled.

Cybersecurity will also slow the uptake of driverless cars. A few years ago, hackers in Saint Louis demonstrated that they could control a vehicle's steering and braking systems via the online entertainment system.[17] This is a challenge facing the Internet of Things (IoT). As the geek joke goes, the "S" in IoT stands for "security." For all our fallibilities and foibles, at least we human drivers are immune to cyberattacks.

Even if it can all be made to work, the technology is still prohibitively expensive. A lidar system that allows an artificial intelligence to monitor the road currently costs in excess of $50,000. And that is just one of the components of a self-driving vehicle. Eventually, investment bank UBS forecasts that the cost per mile to travel in a driverless car could drop to $0.70, below the current cost of a private car ($1.20 per mile) or ride-hailing service ($2.50 per mile).[18] But as the job optimists point out, it will take time before driverless vehicles are cheaper than driven ones.

Finally, technologies have a way of exposing what is really valuable about people. The term "driver" suggests that people are valued for their driving skills. But truck drivers also protect their load, troubleshoot problems, and ensure they are dealing with the right people at each end of the journey. Of the four million employed in the United States as drivers, three million drive trucks. If we still need humans to drive the first and last ten miles of every journey, then many of these people will keep their jobs. Indeed, Uber thinks there may be more people employed as truckers in the future than there are today.[19]

Change is coming, but it may take longer to get here than the breathless hype or fear suggests. And it may come in some places and industries well before others. In Australia, iron ore miners BHP and Rio Tinto are both operating driverless trucks. Because they operate in a controlled environment, the firms already bear responsibility for accidents. On public roads, driverless cars and trucks will take longer to replace existing vehicles.

Job optimists like to note that cars once required three drivers. In Britain, the "Red Flag Act" of 1865 regulated self-propelled vehicles, dubbed "locomotives." The law stated that "at least three persons shall be employed to drive or conduct such locomotive." One steered the car, one walked at least sixty yards in front carrying a red flag, and the third person helped those who might be affected by the sight or noise of the automobile. When the Red Flag Act was repealed in 1896, the numbers of drivers per car fell from three to one.

Job optimists also like to point out that the move from horse to car travel did not lead to mass joblessness. In 1900, there were fifteen million horses in the United States. A century later, there were only three million. As cars replaced horses, the number of people working as farriers, saddle makers, and stable hands decreased. But because the change took place steadily, those affected were able to move into other employment. The invention of the automobile put most of the horses out of work, but the people responsible for those horses found other employment. The difference? Humans could be retrained to work in emerging occupations. Horses couldn't.

The same is true of agriculture more generally. Since 1900, the share of the US population involved in agriculture has fallen from 40 to 2 percent. Fewer people now work in the farm sector than at the start of the last century, yet the real value of agricultural output has nearly tripled. Go to a modern farm today, and you'll see how chemistry has changed what animals are fed, how GPS software has changed how crops are harvested, and how drones are improving farmers' ability to see what's going on in the far corners of their properties. Technology has made agriculture far more productive—but it hasn't created many jobs.

Millions of agricultural jobs have been lost, yet people have found new vocations. Since the end of World War II, unemployment has averaged around 6 percent, topping 8 percent on only three occasions: the mid-1970s, the early-1980s, and the great recession. Admittedly, there are also some people who do not show up in the unemployment statistics because they have stopped actively seeking work. But even so, the technological revolution in agriculture has not led to rampant job losses.

There is no grand economic theory that tells us why the number of horses in the US economy shrank by four-fifths over the twentieth century, while the number of workers grew sixfold.[20] Yet the job optimists can point to numerous instances where things worked out better than the doomsayers feared. There are plenty of historical moments in which innovation has not led to the feared dystopia.

Optimists argue that machines often act as tools that free up people from those tasks, and allow them to concentrate on more fruitful and productive areas. Their advice to those worried about displacement is to think about why your past experience may give you leverage in the new jobs created when automated tools appear. These tools can create superpowers, but the superpowers are frequently given to people.

Humans may end up working with new technologies in unexpected ways.[21] Google employs ten thousand "raters" for tasks such as testing new services and checking questionable YouTube videos. Facebook employs twenty thousand moderators.[22] Amazon's Mechanical Turk pays around five hundred thousand people for performing simple tasks that computers cannot yet do, such as accurately transcribing audio files. One start-up, CrowdFlower, specializes in answering email queries. Incoming requests are first sent to an algorithm, which can answer most questions. Only when the algorithm is stumped is the query sent to a human. A key policy challenge is ensuring that these new jobs are quality jobs—an issue we will return to below.

In practice, it can be difficult to use technology to eliminate jobs, since innovations create unexpected new roles. Surgeon Atul Gawande examined the adoption of new computer systems inside hospitals designed to record data more accurately, eliminate paper, and improve health outcomes.[23] The process was far from seamless. Physicians were frustrated as they struggled to enter information in the new systems. Patients found that their doctors spent much of the time in appointments reading from a computer screen or tapping on a keyboard. That said, the system did actually improve health outcomes in areas where the sharing of information was important (e.g., identifying people at risk from opioid abuse). Eventually, to balance these trade-offs, hospitals found a new solution: they employed "scribes" to shadow physicians and enter information on the fly. The demand for these was so high that some hospitals developed systems that allowed these tasks to be performed remotely by scribes in India. How hospitals of the future will manage technology is uncertain, but it does show how innovations can create unexpected jobs.

One area where there have long been forecasts of job destruction is retailing, where self-checkouts and the growth in e-commerce has caused brick-and-mortar stores to scale back. In the mid-1980s, Sears was the biggest retailer in the United States. In 2018, it filed for bankruptcy. Other retailers that have filed for bankruptcy in recent years include Toys"R"Us, Brookstone, RadioShack, Payless, and Nine West.

But bankruptcy for retailers need not mean joblessness for their workers. In 2016, Belinda Duperre, who sold jewelry at the low-cost retailer Sam's Club, lost her job when the store shut down.[24] Not long afterward, Amazon opened up a large fulfillment center in her town. Duperre was hired in the new facility. Her new job—packing boxes on high-speed conveyer belts—was more physical, but also paid two dollars an hour more than her old job.

This may not be the end of the story for Duperre. After all, Amazon is hardly the world's most congenial workplace, and the company is constantly looking to automate its processes.[25] Every year it holds the Amazon Picking Challenge, which has robotics teams compete to come up with automated solutions to one of the company's biggest problems: how to pick up desired objects and place them in boxes. Robots have been successful in automating much of the packing process, but picking eludes them.

At present, because humans are much better at identifying objects than computers, Amazon's Kiva book-packing system uses both robots and humans. When you order a book, Amazon's robots fetch the relevant bookshelf from the warehouse and bring it to the packing area. The shelves aren't classified alphabetically; instead, items are stored along with others that are likely to be bought by the same customer. But the last step—taking the right book off the shelf and packing it—is done by a human. Everything else is organized by machines, but that last task is squarely a human enterprise.

Job optimists see the opportunities for humans as potentially limitless. Job pessimists are worried that Duperre's luck will run out. As we write this book, companies such as Vancouver's Kindred are investing heavily in finding a way to automate picking. They do so by having humans hooked up to simulators that control robots in factories. Robots observe the choices made by the people, and the goal is that they will become trained to do picking independently. But there is an alternative scenario whereby the robots are employed at fulfillment centers and humans remotely control them. In that case, for people like Duperre, new technology may allow them to remove some of the luck out of their job search and work from wherever they live. Potentially, technology could raise the incomes—net of housing costs—of these workers. In the two and a half centuries since the Industrial Revolution, the labor market has continued to evolve. Yet there are still enough jobs available for almost everyone who wants one. Under the optimistic scenario, the jobs of the future will be different but plentiful.

The Job Pessimists

One of the most famous ideas in science fiction is the *singularity*: the notion of a turning point when computers become capable of recursive self-improvement. Unlike human generations, which last around thirty years, computer generations are almost instantaneous. So even if a computer is only making a small improvement each generation, the power of the system would quickly take off.

The concern is that it would be our last invention. This "intelligence explosion" would rapidly lead to computers whose capacity was beyond our understanding and control. Once superintelligent machines surpass the ability of humans, we might expect them to be more inventive than Albert Einstein, to compose music better than Wolfgang Amadeus Mozart, to invest better than Buffett, and write plays superior to William Shakespeare. After all, amazing as those individuals were, they were still limited by a three-pound brain with a hundred billion neurons. One researcher compares the singularity to the "Cambrian Explosion" half a billion years ago, when creatures suddenly evolved that could see, and within a short time frame, life on earth was transformed.[26]

Those who have expressed concern about the impact of the singularity on humans include Elon Musk, who calls artificial intelligence "summoning

the demon." The late Stephen Hawking wrote, "One can imagine such technology outsmarting financial markets, out-inventing human researchers,
out-manipulating human leaders, and developing weapons we cannot even
understand."[27] Even Bill Gates has questioned whether enough is being done
to avert the potential dangers of the singularity. Musk, Hawking, and Gates
can hardly be said to lack a solid understanding of artificial intelligence.

While some argue that superintelligent computers might happily coexist
with humans, others fear a future like the scenario depicted in *Terminator*,
in which the Skynet artificial intelligence system becomes self-aware
and initiates a nuclear holocaust, followed by a war between humans and
machines. Swedish philosopher Nick Bostrom gives the example of computers that merely wanted to make as many paper clips as possible.[28] Pretty
quickly, Bostrom cautions, our cars and homes could find themselves
becoming fodder for them. As he points out, the chief concern isn't that
machines would be hostile or evil. Instead, the problem is that it is hard to
imagine computers having a set of preferences that would positively affect
our well-being. We aren't sure this dire scenario will play out, but it has
influenced many in becoming worried about artificial intelligence.[29] Even if
machines could be engineered so as to pursue only goals that made humans
better off, how confident could we be that they would stick with these goals
as they "evolved"?

In his science fiction novel *Accelerando*, Charles Stross points out that
the chances of people catching up to the machines after the singularity
is virtually nil. As one character wryly observes, "Humans are just barely
intelligent tool users; Darwinian evolutionary selection stopped when language and tool use converged, leaving the average hairy meme carrier sadly
deficient in smarts."[30]

Stross's novel offers a list of answers to "Frequently Asked Questions"
that might be asked by "humanoids." It reads in part, "While many things
are free, it is highly likely that you possess no employable skills, and therefore, no way of earning money with which to purchase unfree items. The
pace of change in the past century has rendered almost all skills you may
have learned obsolete [see singularity]. However, owing to the rapid pace of
change, many cooperatives, trusts, and guilds offer on-the-job training or
educational loans."[31]

That said, neither of us wake up in the middle of the night worrying
about the singularity. Ever since the 1950s, such a breakthrough in artificial

intelligence has always been twenty to thirty years away. This is just close enough to feel attainable, but not so near that a research funding body will be disappointed if you fail to reach the goal within the term of your grant. Appropriately enough, a survey of participants at the 2012 Singularity Summit returned a median estimate of 2040.[32]

But if you're a highly educated reader who is confident that your work could never be replicated by a machine, then you should take a moment to ponder the singularity. That's because it will put you in the shoes of those who are already being replaced by computers and robots. Thinking about the singularity should make you feel a little more vulnerable. It might even make you a smidgen more sympathetic toward the Luddites of the early 1800s. That's how millions of workers are feeling right now.

Nearly two centuries ago, Ricardo pointed out in his *Principles of Political Economy* that the introduction of robots that could substitute for a worker meant that the equilibrium wage of the worker would come down to the rental price of the machine.[33] Nobel laureate Leontief wrote 150 years later that "any worker who now performs his task by following specific instructions can, in principle, be replaced by a machine. This means that the role of humans as the most important factor of production is bound to diminish—in the same way that the role of horses in agricultural production was first diminished and then eliminated by the introduction of tractors."[34] The forecast is that as robots get cheaper, wages in the equivalent sector will fall. If we're dealing with a superintelligence—a robot that outperforms humans at every conceivable task—that seems to paint a picture whereby everyone's wage falls to zero. That's where the pessimists begin.

What do we know about job loss due to automation so far? For several years, MIT's David Autor has set about trying to understand the changes afoot in the labor market. In a series of articles with not-so-reassuring titles like "Why Are There Still So Many Jobs?" Autor and coauthors have looked at job change by dividing jobs into three categories: manual, routine, and abstract.

Routine jobs are occupations such as data entry, administrative support, and repetitive manufacturing tasks. For example, when Andrew worked as an attorney in the early 1990s, law firms had typing pools—a group of people whose job it was to take recordings from microcassettes, and turn them into well-formatted contracts, letters, and file notes. Such typing pools no longer exist. Right now, café ordering apps such as Ritual are displacing the routine work traditionally done by cashiers. What makes routine jobs vulnerable to computerization is that they involve following established rules. "Put the tape in the recorder. Type up the letter. Save and print." Or, "Scan the customer's order. Take their payment."

By contrast, abstract jobs involve problem solving, creativity, and teamwork. When a lawyer advises a client whether to accept a plea bargain or a manager decides how to respond to an employee arriving late for work, they are tackling problems that do not have a closed-form solution. It is unlikely that computers will replace the work presently done by artists, veterinarians, merchant bankers, architects, physicians, professors, or politicians—at least until the singularity comes along.

More interesting is the resilience of manual jobs to computerization. Despite the predictions of science fiction—from *Star Wars* to the *Jetsons*—attempts to automate the work of jobs such as cooking, cleaning, security work, and personal care have largely failed. For example, researchers at the University of California at Berkeley are working on a robot that can fold laundry. Their prototype can fold a towel in a painfully slow ninety seconds, but finds itself stumped by new items such as socks and shirts.[35]

This challenge of shape recognition has stumped other attempts at automation. Current robot hairdressers produce a result similar to what you'd get if you consumed a bottle of tequila and tried to give yourself a haircut without a mirror.[36] An experiment in cat recognition by Google X labs found that the system incorrectly identified a pair of coffee mugs as a cat. When given the right instructions, modern robots can be incredibly dexterous. The problem is a software, not a hardware, one.[37] The job pessimists point out that it is only a matter of time before the algorithms catch up to our three-pound brains.

Looking across the economy, Autor and coauthors analyze changes in the three categories of abstract, manual, and routine jobs. Consistent with what we have discussed, they find that routine jobs, which tend to fall in the middle of the wage distribution, have shrunk most.[38] This is true in the United States for the 1980s, 1990s, and 2000s.[39] It is also true of most European countries over the period 1993 to 2010.[40]

Another way that researchers have tackled the question is to look not at the future but instead at the past. One study specifically focuses on industrial robots—machines that are automatic, programmable, and multipurpose. This means that your coffee machine isn't an industrial robot (because it can only do one task). In factories today, industrial robots are doing jobs such as welding, assembling, painting, and packing.

Over the past generation, robot use has expanded across the economy, rising from less than half a machine for every 1,000 US workers in 1993 to nearly 2 robots per 1,000 workers in 2015. Naturally, this average includes sectors with no robots as well as sectors where robots are ubiquitous. For example, in the car-manufacturing sector, there are 122 robots for every 1,000 US workers.[41] The International Federation for Robotics estimates that in 2019, the world will have 2.6 robots for every 1,000 workers.

Looking at the spread of industrial robots across the United States, Daron Acemoglu and Pascual Restrepo find that in places where more robots are installed, employment and wages decline substantially. For every new robot, 6 workers lose their jobs. Given that robots are shipping fast—one projection estimates that the worldwide stock of robots could triple to 5 million by 2025—this suggests that robots could displace tens of millions of workers across the globe in the coming years.[42]

Over time, robotic innovations could see the creation of new industries, potentially generating job opportunities that do not exist today. But in the short term, these findings suggest that robots are having a negative impact on employment in the areas where most of them are being installed. When you hear talk about "bringing back manufacturing" to the United States, it's important to bear in mind that they are talking about twenty-first-century manufacturing—not twentieth-century manufacturing. Onshoring means new factories, but not so many jobs.

Similar findings emerge from studies that look at the spread of faster internet. A Norwegian analysis found that broadband internet improves the labor market outcomes and productivity of skilled workers. At the same time, broadband worsens the labor market outcomes and productivity of unskilled Norwegian workers. The authors find suggestive evidence that broadband adoption in firms complements skilled workers in executing nonroutine abstract tasks, and substitutes for unskilled workers in perform-ing routine tasks.[43] Like robots, superfast broadband tends to be bad news for unskilled workers who perform routine jobs.

Some of the characteristics that will be hardest for computers to mimic are those of communicating clearly with coworkers, showing empathy to clients, and adapting to new situations. This indicates that it will be hard to replace security guards, aged-care nurses, or masseuses, at least in the short term. A significant number of manual jobs will be around for the next few decades.

What does this mean for wages? Because job loss has been concentrated at the middle of the distribution, people have referred to its effect of "polarizing" or "hollowing out" the labor market. Some have mistakenly inferred that because the occupations where jobs are lost have been at the middle, therefore the pain has been most acute for midlevel workers or middle-class households.

The reason that we can't go from an impact on *midlevel jobs* to an impact on *middle-class families* is that we also need to think about labor supply. It's one thing to know that the demand for security guards and dog walkers is booming. But because these occupations require relatively little training, the supply of workers is also high. As workers in middle-paid jobs have become redundant, they have cascaded down to compete with those in low-paid jobs. The net result is that for those in the bottom half of the US wage distribution, earnings after inflation aren't much higher than they were in the *Brady Bunch* era.

At the top, it's an altogether-different tale, with technology augmenting the skills of the most skillful. One of the professions that is making use of technology is surgery, where the old-fashioned notion of a lone expert is being replaced by integrated teams that rely heavily on computers and robots. For operations such as total knee replacement, the best surgical teams now use computer guidance to help them determine precisely what angle to cut the bone. Computer guidance means that the new knee works better and is less likely to require remedial surgery. That in turn means that more people will want to get their knees replaced. Which means more demand for the services of top surgeons.

In coming years, robotic devices may even make the cuts, mix the adhesive cement, and fit the prosthesis. Firms such as Cambridge Medical Robotics, Intuitive Surgical, and Medical Microinstruments are developing new surgical robots that could enable operations that are currently too delicate for humans to safely perform, such as on premature babies and tiny tumors.[44]

The same is true of the world's best architects, who are now designing buildings that would have been impossible before the computer age. Frank Gehry's iconic Guggenheim Museum in Bilbao was only feasible because Gehry's firm adapted French aerospace software to create the detailed construction plans.[45] New software allows architects to model the heating and cooling costs, allowing designers to create more environmentally efficient buildings.

Let's take another category of abstract workers. For CEOs, one of the drivers of increasing pay has been that the biggest firms have gotten bigger. This is partly a technology story. Managers have benefited from advances in travel technology, communications technology, data analytics, and systems integration, which make it possible to run bigger firms than ever before. Researchers have shown that a CEO's salary is proportional to the size of the firm.[46] So technological advances that make it easier for managers to coordinate larger and larger enterprises also increase earnings in the corner office.

Another reason that job pessimists worry about the impact of innovation is that other factors are also increasing US inequality. Since 1970, the unionization rate has fallen from a quarter to a tenth.[47] Because unions campaign for pay equity across and within workplaces, a lower unionization rate means more inequality.[48] It isn't easy to separate declining union membership rates from inequality, with some research suggesting that technological change may be one of the factors reducing unionization.[49]

Institutions matter too. Adjusted for inflation, the federal minimum wage was $11.79 in 1968, compared with $7.25 today.[50] A lower minimum wage means more wage inequality. Meanwhile, high earners have benefited considerably from changes in federal policies. Over the same period, the top personal income tax rate was halved from 75.25 percent in 1968 to 37 percent today. Lower top tax rates increase inequality in disposable incomes. But because those at the top save a significant share of their incomes, lower tax rates also increase the pretax incomes of top income earners in future years.[51]

The impact of trade and migration on US inequality is more contested. While trade theory suggests that the largest gains are to be made when countries with very different economies exchanged goods and services, it turned out that for much of the postwar era, global trade tended to be between advanced nations. For example, in 1990, the top sources of US imports were Canada, Japan, Mexico, Germany, and the United Kingdom. On average, countries from which the United States drew its imports paid wages that were 81 percent of the US average.[52] The value of US manufacturing imports from advanced countries in 1990 was twice as large as the value of imports from developing nations.

Not surprisingly, then, when economists in the 1990s estimated the impact of imports on inequality, they didn't find much. Using data up to the early 1990s, the leading studies which looked at the impact of trade on the wage gap between skilled and unskilled workers estimated that its effect was only 1 to 3 percentage points.[53]

Over the next quarter century, the composition of US trade changed dramatically. Rapid economic growth in the "tigers" (Hong Kong, Singapore, South Korea, and Taiwan) and "tiger cubs" (Indonesia, Malaysia, the Philippines, and Thailand) saw thousands of factories set up production in Asia. China's accession to the World Trade Organization in 2001 turbocharged its model of export-led growth. By 2005, the average wage in countries from which the United States got its imports was down to 65 percent of the US average. In 2007, China overtook Canada as the largest source of imports for the United States, and today accounts for more than one-fifth of US imports.[54] The benefit to households can be seen in just about every store and home in the United States: a plethora of affordable consumer products marked "Made in China."

Because some of these products supplanted items formerly made in the United States, trade with China probably explains about one-quarter of the decline in manufacturing employment.[55] The regions of the United States most exposed to trade with China have seen larger wage falls and higher levels of welfare receipt. But the jobs that disappeared as a result would likely have been lost due to automation. What trade did was to bring forward those job losses by fifteen to twenty years.[56]

In the case of immigration, there is still considerable disagreement among economists. While it is true that immigrants can take jobs that would otherwise have been filled by native-born workers, they also create jobs. Immigrants are more than twice as likely to start a business as people born in the United States.[57] Specialist visas mean that many documented migrants fill a critical role in a company. Because immigrants are consumers too, they help to provide additional employment opportunities for locals. And one point that all economists agree on is that migration from developing to developed nations massively boosts the incomes of migrants themselves.

Empirical studies that have looked across cities to see the impacts of migration on local workers have found scant evidence that an influx of immigrants drives down the wages of low-skilled employees.[58] But as critics have pointed out, this might be because locals are simply moving elsewhere. Using differences in skill groups across the country, one study reported that immigration from 1980 to 2000 increased the wage gap between high school dropouts and college graduates by 4 percent.[59] Yet even if this larger estimate is right, it still suggests that immigration is a much less important driver of inequality than technology.

Just as the rapid growth in Chinese trade brought forward the labor market disruption that would have occurred from automation, so too the impact of immigration has been to accelerate the technology sector. One-third of US Nobel laureates are immigrants.[60] More than half of all billion-dollar start-ups were founded by immigrants, and over two-thirds employ immigrants in crucial executive roles.[61] By helping to create firms such as Google, Tesla, and Uber, immigrants have sped up the rate at which technology is changing the economy. One-quarter of the nation's innovation workforce are migrants.[62] This isn't a new phenomenon; a study of innovative nineteenth-century migrants such as Nikola Tesla found that they "crowded in" local inventors, boosting patenting rates among the native-born population.[63]

In any analysis of advanced country inequality, it's clear that trade and immigration play second fiddle to technological forces. One statistic that sums this up is that over the period 1995 to 2005, the United States lost three million manufacturing jobs. Meanwhile, China lost over ten million manufacturing jobs.[64] During those years, technological advances cost over three times as many Chinese jobs as US ones. As Harvard's Larry Katz encapsulates the impact of globalization versus innovation, "Over the long haul, clearly automation's been much more important—it's not even close."[65]

Job Uncertainty

Humans desperately want to know the future. We watch the weather channel to find out if it will rain tomorrow. We track opinion polls to find out who will win elections. Sports pundits make a living discussing who will win the next game. If we get a bad medical diagnosis, the first question we ask is, "How long have I got, doctor?"

With such a strong demand for forecasts, it's not surprising that some people have claimed that they can predict which jobs are going to disappear. A study by Oxford researchers Carl Frey and Michael Osborne looks at the characteristics of jobs that have been computerized, and attempts to model the likelihood that particular occupations will be rendered redundant.[66]

The researchers' widely reported conclusion is that 47 percent of jobs *could* be automated. Tabulating over seven hundred occupations, they conclude that the most automatable job is telemarketers (99 percent), while the least automatable job is recreational therapy (less than 1 percent chance).

There are good reasons, however, to be skeptical about the methodology of the Oxford study.[67] In consultation with experts, Frey and Osborne begin by hand coding seventy occupations as being automatable or nonautomatable. Using the US Bureau of Labor Statistics' measures of job characteristics, they then identify the characteristics associated with their automation measures and use this to assign all seven hundred occupational categories a probability of automation. The problem with this approach is that it depends crucially on the way they hand coded the first seventy occupations. For example, Frey and Osborne classify accountants and marketing specialists as occupations that can be automated. But employment in these two job categories has grown strongly in recent years, and it is easier to see such occupations evolving rather than dying.

It's certainly true that some accountants and marketers—perhaps those responsible for routine tasks—will see their jobs disappear. Some professions, such as data entry keyers, securities brokerage clerks, and real estate title examiners, are already under direct threat. But Frey and Osborne's approach doesn't allow for such subtlety. They model occupational change as an all-or-nothing process: either an occupation disappears or it does not. Subsequent studies are more nuanced—breaking this down to a task level.[68]

Moreover, whether a job *will* actually be automated depends not just on its characteristics but also on the relative cost of people and machines.[69] The day that someone invents a superrobot that can do your job is not the day you get fired. You'll keep your job if renting the machine costs more than paying your salary. Even if the machine is cheaper, you may keep your job because customers prefer dealing with a real person. Do you want to put your child into the first robot-run day care center? Would a computerized bartender empathize with your woes? Would you trust an automated hairdresser to know what "Let's try something different" means? In short, the world of automation may be further off than the doomsayers are telling us.

A subtler approach to forecasts is that taken by the Bureau of Labor Statistics. Using past trends, it lists the jobs that it expects to be the fastest growing and shrinking.[70] Growing occupations range from workers installing rooftop solar panels (forecast to grow by 105 percent from 2016 to 2026) to

Fastest-Growing Occupations	Fastest-Shrinking Occupations
Solar photovoltaic installers	Locomotive firers
Wind turbine service technicians	Respiratory therapy technicians
Home health aides	Parking enforcement workers
Personal care aides	Word processors and typists
Physician assistants	Watch repairers
Nurse practitioners	Electronic equipment installers and repairers, motor vehicles
Statisticians	Foundry mold and core makers
Physical therapist assistants	Pourers and casters, metal
Software developers, applications	Computer operators
Mathematicians	Telephone operators
Physical therapist aides	Mine shuttle car operators
Bicycle repairers	Electromechanical equipment assemblers
Medical assistants	Data entry keyers
Genetic counselors	Postmasters and mail superintendents
Occupational therapy assistants	Electric and electronic equipment assemblers
Information security analysts	Coil winders, tapers, and finishers
Physical therapists	Grinding and polishing workers, hand
Operations research analysts	Timing device assemblers and adjusters
Forest fire inspectors and prevention specialists	Switchboard operators, including answering service
Massage therapists	Prepress technicians and workers

massage therapists (forecast to grow by 26 percent). Shrinking occupations range from locomotive firers (forecast to shrink by 79 percent) to prepress technicians (forecast to shrink by 20 percent).

Recall Knight's distinction between risk (not knowing whether you'll pull out a crisp or rotten apple) and uncertainty (not knowing the mix of apples in the bag). Underpinning precise occupational forecasts is the assumption that we're only dealing with risk. That assumes we know which occupations will shrink and grow—and the question is only which particular people will lose and gain jobs.

But the history of occupational forecasting should give us a little more modesty. As Harvard's Richard Freeman points out, past forecasts of the US labor market have turned out to be wildly inaccurate. Freeman gives the example of computer programmers, where demand outstripped forecasters' expectations in the late 1990s, but grew more slowly than forecast in the early 2000s. Freeman notes that forecasters tend to assume that changes are gradual. In practice, changes are more often sudden.[71]

Forecasting also tends to favor the job pessimists. Put yourself back in the year 2000, and imagine you had to forecast what would happen to the US labor market in the coming decades. Maybe you would predict a fall in the numbers of lighthouse keepers and level crossing attendants. But would you have anticipated the rise of app developers, data miners, and social media managers? In practice, it's invariably easier to pinpoint the sectors where jobs will be lost than those in which new positions will be created.

One of the hardest things to know about technological change is the way it might create new job openings. When we replaced human lift operators with automatic elevators, it suddenly became much more affordable to build skyscrapers—creating thousands more openings for construction workers. When we replaced horses with cars, our city streets stopped being filled with manure, which was not only good for public health, but also for street vendors and open-air restaurants. Since then, most of the job creation has occurred in urban areas. Similarly, one of the toughest things to know about driverless cars is how they might create new jobs as they reshape logistics, reduce congestion, and transform the commuter experience.

For this reason, we can learn something from both the job optimists and job pessimists. Both those concerned and those relaxed about disruptions that might arise from the intended use of new technologies have strong arguments. If we are successful in creating innovations, the destruction price may come due. New technologies will replace some of today's jobs. But as the optimists show, new jobs tend to show up elsewhere—sometimes as an unexpected result of the new innovations.

When there is fundamental uncertainty, we can't precisely predict how to put displaced workers in a position to take advantage of new job opportunities. Fortunately, as we discuss below, smart human capital policies have the potential to boost both innovation and equality. Just as individuals take out insurance policies to guard against the risk of a car crash or house fire, so too society needs to think about social insurance policies that suit an uncertain future.

4 Does Innovation Require Inequality?

Growing up in the 1970s, we watched far too many television shows about superheroes. For hours, we followed the on-screen exploits of figures such as Wonder Woman, Superman, Spiderman, and the Hulk. Created in the middle of the twentieth century, these comic book characters had abilities that made them terrifying to criminals. They could fly, fight, and climb walls. They had amazing eyesight, fast reflexes, and a high threshold for pain.

Yet it's worth thinking for a moment about what these superheroes would do for a job in today's labor market. Their superpowers are essentially geared for the industrial era. In the labor market of two generations ago, they could have done well. But in today's labor market, strength is less important than ever. Only one in seven jobs require what the Bureau of Labor Statistics judges to be heavy work."[1] Wages in brawny occupations such as building laborers, security guards, and delivery workers have stagnated over recent decades. It's tough for a tough guy to earn an above-average wage in the modern labor market.

To earn a superwage today requires different superpowers. The best performers aren't surly loners; they're people who can build diverse teams. They're creative and thoughtful. They can communicate effectively, combine ideas in unexpected ways, and engage with statistics, mathematics, and science. The era of *Superman* is over. *Star Trek* provides more insights.

To some people, one of today's new superheroes is Mark Zuckerberg. Since founding Facebook in his Harvard dormitory in 2004, Zuckerberg has grown the social network to over two billion active monthly users worldwide and a market value of over $450 billion. Facebook has over thirty-three thousand employees, and its users spend an average of twenty minutes per day on the site.

Facebook also has its downsides. Just as older communication technologies have facilitated the spread of disinformation and hate speech, so has Facebook. Like many businesses handling personal information, it has been implicated in serious data breaches. Some regard Zuckerberg as more of a supervillain than a superhero. So we should be wary not to overstate Facebook's benefits. Nonetheless, using time spent on the site as our guide, we can conservatively price its value using the US minimum wage at $2 per user per day, or $730 annually (using the average global wage produces a similar figure).[2]

Globally, that suggests that the annual consumer value of the network might be $1.5 trillion. Zuckerberg and his family have over $50 billion as a result of this. Suffice it to say, if there is a reward for successful entrepreneurship and innovation in today's economy, Zuckerberg has received it, and the creation price of that is much less than the benefits its users receive.

But even in this case, where the social value of the innovation was so much greater than the price, we can still ask whether the price was too high. That $50 billion creation price is approximately equivalent to the value of *all* real estate in small US states such as Delaware or Vermont.[3] This should give us enough pause to ask whether it really needed to be paid.

How much money would have induced the innovation that created Facebook? Let's take our cue from *The Social Network*, the 2010 Aaron Sorkin movie, in which one friend said to Zuckerberg, "You don't even know what the thing is yet. How big it can get, how far it can go. This is no time to take your chips down. A million dollars isn't cool, you know what's cool? … A billion dollars." In other words, suppose that Zuckerberg earned a billion dollars from his work on Facebook to date—that's fifty times less than what he did earn. It is certainly plausible that Zuckerberg would have still chosen to drop out of Harvard, move to Silicon Valley, and develop Facebook in much the same way.

We have another clue that Zuckerberg could have been quite satisfied with a billion dollars. In December 2015, the day after the birth of their first child, Zuckerberg and his spouse, Priscilla Chan, pledged to donate 99 percent of their Facebook shares to a charitable initiative focused on health and education. On today's valuation, they would leave themselves with half a billion dollars. In so doing, Zuckerberg reduced his own creation price to a fraction of that amount he could have been paid.

We must admit that this characterization is itself simplistic, since Zuckerberg and Chan receive satisfaction from benefaction. But the magnitudes involved suggest that Zuckerberg didn't need a creation price of $50 billion. And Zuckerberg is far from the first entrepreneur to donate their creation price. As of 2019, 190 major philanthropists were listed as part of the Giving Pledge.[4] This was an organization founded by Bill and Melinda Gates and Warren Buffett with the goal of convincing billionaires to donate much of their fortunes. The total pledge to date is in excess of $400 billion (including the pledge of Zuckerberg and Chan). Most givers pledge a majority of their wealth.

The creation price says that a certain amount of wealth needs to be given to successful innovators to ensure they take the decisions to generate those innovations. Naturally, this goes beyond the personal wealth of entrepreneurs, and also is a reward to those who risk capital in pursuit of technological advance as founders or investors. But it is precisely because that wealth is concentrated among the relatively few who are successful innovators that the level of the creation price is relevant to whether the fruits of their activities are affordable. That is, if the fruits of wealth creation could otherwise be shared among more households, the hopes of many more people would be affordable. If spreading the wealth associated with high creation prices undermines the innovations that created greater wealth in the first place, however, those other people's hopes would not be affordable.

In this chapter, we consider in more detail the logic behind the view that innovation requires inequality. We then look to the evidence to see whether it is likely that innovation rates would be harmed by a more equal distribution of wealth. At the end of the chapter, we discuss the significant role that governments play in spurring innovation.

The Reward Argument

There are, basically, two arguments for why inequality is worth it as the creation price for progress. One is a risk argument that states that inequality is required so that those who hold capital assets have an incentive to deploy them toward innovative ends. We will discuss that shortly. First, we focus on the reward argument: that inequality is necessary to generate incentives for talented people to become entrepreneurs.

The reward argument can often be appealing because it is put forward by those who are otherwise skeptical of the level of inequality. For instance, former US treasury secretary Larry Summers asserted that if the United States could have thirty more people like Jobs, it would be a good thing even at the expense of increased inequality.[5] This is despite the fact that he was not sure that Jobs's and Apple's innovations had created more middle-class jobs in the US.

A similar take on this comes from Paul Graham, who is the cofounder of a successful Silicon Valley accelerator, Y Combinator. Graham contends that "almost by definition, if a startup succeeds its founders become rich. And while getting rich is not the only goal of most startup founders, few would do it if one couldn't."[6] Graham sees himself as a "manufacturer of inequality" because he teaches start-ups how to get rich. Whether this is the case or not is something we will return to in the next chapter. Without substantial monetary rewards, he believes that Silicon Valley would not flourish.

As we noted earlier, these arguments relate to the notion that you do not have to worry if someone has a bigger slice of the pie if they are responsible for producing a bigger pie. But again, we need to emphasize that it is not sufficient to observe rich entrepreneurs who have produced socially valuable innovations and infer that the subsequent level of their richness was a necessary condition for their innovative choices. Even Graham seems to understand this, writing, "If you want to understand *change* in economic inequality, you should ask what those people would have done when it was different."[7] Precisely.

As we already maintained, this is where analysis becomes tricky. For entrepreneurs like Zuckerberg, who choose to give their wealth away, we have to ask what they would have done differently had it been taxed rather than donated? But for others like Jobs, who did not donate his wealth to philanthropy, there is a similar puzzle. By all accounts he lived relatively modestly. In which case, we have to ask, Was the reward just a number in a bank account?

But Jobs represents a puzzle on another dimension. While many hold him up as an example of why we need inequality to get innovation, Jobs, who created one of the world's most valuable companies, did not receive the majority of his wealth directly from Apple. Reports vary, but when he passed away in 2011, he left his family $7 billion. Of that, less than $1 billion was in the form of Apple shares. Why did Jobs have so few Apple shares?

When he was ousted from the company in 1985, he sold his stake. When he returned in 1997, he did not gather a significant number of shares or options. Jobs did his innovating without the financial reward that accrues to today's successful start-ups.

However, the central question doesn't come down to individuals. Instead, we need to ask how many choose to take risks and become entrepreneurs because of the prospects of securing a Zuckerberg- or Gates-like fortune? The idea is to ensure that entrepreneurs have enough of a potential payoff so that the next Zuckerberg doesn't go and work as a dentist, and the next Jobs does not become a debt collector.[8]

As we will discuss below, innovation goes well beyond the rarified worlds of Harvard dropouts like Zuckerberg and Gates. But let's stick with that milieu for a moment since it has attracted considerable attention among those who contend that the secret to producing more entrepreneurs is to lighten the tax load on billionaires.

Imagine that someone who just graduated from a university could secure a job on Wall Street earning them a total of half a million dollars over their first five years. If they instead pursued a start-up, suppose that they had a certain probability of ending up with a so-called unicorn business worth $1 billion at the end of five years, but otherwise earning nothing if it failed. Finally, just to keep things simple, imagine that the start-up option does not harm the person's earning power after five years. So long as they aren't risk averse, a little math tells us that this person will choose to be an entrepreneur rather than a Wall Streeter so long as their likelihood of entrepreneurial success is at least one in two thousand.[9] That may seem like a small number, but there are few entrepreneurs who walk away as billionaires, and so it should not surprise you that far fewer graduates choose to become entrepreneurs compared to taking on more stable jobs like Wall Street traders.

This reasoning also tells us why taxation arguments that are designed to deal with inequality are subtle. In our example, both the Wall Street trader and the entrepreneur will find themselves on the top marginal tax rate in many countries. That means that the same proportion of their income will be given over to tax authorities by the end of five years. So if that tax rate is 30 percent, applying equally to both kinds of earnings, then the Wall Street trader will pay almost $150,000 in tax while an entrepreneur who successfully creates a unicorn business will pay almost $300 million in tax.

What the mathematics tells us in this instance is that the graduate's decision is unchanged. The same one in two thousand success threshold guides their decision.[10] Absent risk aversion, when the government is taking a share of your income as taxes, this does not change major career decisions. It is only if the tax rate is *higher* for the entrepreneur than the trader that the tax system might change the decision to become an entrepreneur. If success in entrepreneurship is taxed at a higher rate than other, more secure income, graduates may choose to forgo entrepreneurship because of the tax system.

Even this is a stretch, though. To see this, we note that the search for a unicorn start-up is akin to the search for alien life. In 1961, astronomer Frank Drake wanted to estimate the likely number of civilizations in our galaxy, the Milky Way. He did this by multiplying the number of stars by the probability that those stars had planets by the probability that those planets could support life and so on, all the way to how long a civilization might last, and whether it is likely to be around now. In this case, even if you start with a large number—such as the hundred to four hundred billion stars in the Milky Way—the multiplication of probabilities shrinks things down to pretty low numbers. He ended up guesstimating the number of likely civilizations at around a hundred (in case you're excited by this number, the nearest likely candidate is twenty-five trillion miles away).[11] Put simply, even with huge numbers of stars, and lots of planets that could house life, the probability that they have a civilization is low. That translates into relatively tiny quantities.

We can apply this same multiplicative logic to start-up returns. If you take $1 billion and multiply it by the fraction of that not owed to the government in taxes you get $700 million for a 30 percent tax rate. If the probability of actually founding a start-up worth that much was one in two thousand (which is generous), then what you really expect to earn is $350,000, or 1/2000th of $700 million. If we raise the tax rate to 40 percent, your expected earnings are $300,000. In other words, it is the fact that creating such unicorns is so rare—hence their name—that limits the anticipated monetary rewards from entrepreneurship. For would-be entrepreneurs, the odds of becoming a unicorn matter more than the tax rate on unicorns.

While stylized, this example helps us frame the strongest form of the reward argument. It is not an argument about tax rates on the rich. People with talents that are in demand from the market are likely to become rich regardless. Thus, the tax rate on the rich plays little role in the path they choose to become rich.

While tax rates may not matter to a graduate deciding to pursue entrepreneurship or a highly paid trading job, tax loopholes could. Assume that our hypothetical graduate is not only rational and risk neutral, but also perfectly informed about the tax code. In that case, if the tax system provides more tax breaks to traders than to entrepreneurs, then the success threshold for entrepreneurship will need to improve before the graduate will take a chance on starting a business. Conversely, if the tax loopholes favor entrepreneurs, it will tilt the decision toward entrepreneurship—meaning the graduate will be more willing to try entrepreneurship, even if it is a long shot.

At the extreme, if the tax breaks are so generous that the trader avoids tax entirely, then the odds of success required for our hypothetical graduate to choose the entrepreneurial path fall from a threshold of one in two thousand to one in fourteen hundred.[12] In effect, a tax code that favors traders over entrepreneurs means that people will be less inclined to chase start-ups that are a long shot. Conversely, if the tax code puts a 30 percent tax on traders but allows entrepreneurs to avoid all taxes, then a would-be entrepreneur only needs a success probability of one in twenty-eight hundred to find this path attractive.[13] Naturally, this ignores the many other arguments against tax loopholes, which can distort behavior, undermine the sense of fairness in the system, and lead to gross inequities.

So that's the theoretical story, assuming we're dealing with a graduate who's hyperrational, fully informed, and doesn't worry about risk. But what does the evidence show on how much these monetary incentives and prospects say about the propensity of graduates to become entrepreneurs? If we reduce the tax rate on the very successful, how many more Jobses can we expect to get?

Perhaps the most careful analysis of this question is a study by Ufuk Akcigit, John Grigsby, Tom Nicholas, and Stefanie Stantcheva, who look at whether changes in state tax rates affect the number of patents filed in that state.[14] Using data from across the twentieth century, and applying a range of careful analytic approaches, they estimate that the effect is large and statistically significant. When a state raises its top income tax rate by 1 percentage point, the number of patents falls by 5 percent. The impact of the corporate income tax cut is slightly larger: a 1 percentage point increase in the company tax rate lowers the number of patents by 5 percent. The authors give the example of New York State's decision to significantly increase taxes in 1968. Before the change, patent rates in New York track those in California quite closely. After the tax rise, New York patent rates fell significantly behind.

While the study is impressive, we do not regard it as the last word on the topic of innovation and taxation. While patent filings are often used as a proxy for innovation, most inventions are not patented. Just three technology categories—information and communication technologies, medical technologies, and pharmaceuticals—account for more than half of all US patents.[15] Some innovators rely on alternative forms of intellectual property protection, particularly copyright. More commonly still, innovators depend on secrecy, with even research-intensive firms reporting that they are more likely to use trade secrets than patents to protect their ideas.[16]

Another limitation of the research is that it is tricky to identify whether higher taxes are reducing overall patenting rates or merely causing inventors to shift to low-tax states. Akcigit and coauthors attempt to address this by showing specifications that exclude "movers." They are only able to define movers, however, as those who file patents in more than one state. If inventors move to a low-tax jurisdiction before filing their first patent, they would not be counted as a mover.

From an individual state's perspective, all this might not matter much, but from an overall standpoint, the distinction is critical. We know from other research that inventors look at tax rates when considering whether to move interstate.[17] If tax cuts are simply shifting patents around the country rather than spurring fresh innovation, then there is a risk that a "race to the bottom" on state taxes may not make the United States a more inventive nation. If the true price of a state tax cut is that schools have less money to attract math and science teachers, the long-term cost will likely outweigh any short-term gain.[18] A similar issue arises with "patent boxes"—a corporate tax break that has been adopted by several nations in recent years. Research suggests that this tax concession leads only to an increase in opportunistic patent filings as opposed to boosting true economic activity.[19]

Are the decisions of graduates at top universities predominantly driven by financial rewards? When Pian Shu read President Barack Obama's assertion that "too many potential physicists and engineers spend their careers shifting money around in the financial sector, instead of applying their talents to innovating in the real economy," she decided to test the theory.[20]

With finance becoming more mathematical, and up to one-third of graduates from the most elite colleges choosing finance as their career path, Obama's concerns seemed well founded.

While it is true that financial careers are financially lucrative, Shu found that the money did not seem to be the primary driver. Studying MIT students, she discovered that finance was the most popular career option. Yet the best science and engineering students were more likely to innovate, and less likely to opt for a job in finance. When Shu studied the career decisions of those at MIT during the great recession, she found that as finance sector wages fell, it was the less academic students who switched their career paths, not the superstars. Shu also saw the same result when she looked at participants in the Putnam competition—an elite mathematics contest for undergraduates. Again, top performers are more likely to go into science and engineering research than take a job in finance.[21]

We should be careful about extrapolating this result too far, but it does suggest that the decision to become an entrepreneur or inventor is not all about the money. Top students are more likely to become innovators. This result indicates that modest increases in taxation at the federal level are unlikely to have a big effect on who chooses an entrepreneurial path.

Impact of Uncertainty

The above statement of the reward argument assumes that people know the odds of success when considering whether to be an entrepreneur. But in reality, how on earth can anyone possibly guess at such a thing?

Whether new creation has an impact is inherently uncertain. It is one of the things that makes an innovation an innovation. Normally, when it comes to uncertainty, we can find some rules of thumb to indicate the likelihood of success. But when it comes to innovation, the overall success rate of entrepreneurs isn't particularly informative. Whether a start-up makes the big time depends much more on the entrepreneur's skills and the specific idea. Going back to Knight's distinction between risk and uncertainty, it's not that the entrepreneur is putting their hand into a bag where they know the mix of crisp and rotten apples. Instead, the entrepreneurial decision may be more akin to figuring out whether the bag contains half or almost all rotten apples. In other words, the problem may be one of uncertainty rather than mere risk.

The uncertainty is so fundamental it can go both ways. When it comes to technological innovations, history is littered with innovations that failed to live up to their promise. Only a few years ago, a Silicon Valley start-up, Lytro, developed a new type of camera. Its field camera captured all the waves of light hitting its sensor, allowing photographers to do something they had only ever dreamed of: focus an image after taking it. This meant they could correct mistakes, or simply sit back later on and work out what objects they would like to highlight. This new design, with its promise to radically change photography, captured the attention of investors, who poured tens of millions of dollars into the company.

Despite early hype, Lytro has struggled. It introduced a mid-range camera that failed to sell due to its low resolution. It then introduced a high-end professional camera that failed to sell due to its slow shutter speed. It tried licensing deals. It moved into video to support new interests in virtual reality. In 2018, the company sold its intellectual property to Google and shut down.

We talked hypothetically about success rates before, but in reality, fundamental uncertainty means that the decision to become an entrepreneur cannot be objectified. It's hard to imagine that we could ever say that someone has a one in a thousand chance of success, while another has a one in a hundred chance. Instead, the prospects of the business are so clouded that they cannot easily factor into calculations. To be sure, if a pernicious government were to impose 100 percent tax rates on the earnings of successful entrepreneurs, it would not matter if there was uncertainty or not; the difference between success and failure would end up being the same. But when we talk about changes to top tax rates that are of the order of a few percent, these changes are unlikely to factor significantly in the decision to become an entrepreneur.

Rather, what is likely to factor strongly is what is known. And what is known are the initial costs that entrepreneurs face in starting ventures and conducting associated research. In other words, compared with changes—even significant ones—in the level of wealth that a successful entrepreneur might earn, lowering the up-front costs of entrepreneurship can induce a greater number of people to take a risk. This leads us to the happy conclusion that the strategy that encourages more innovation is also an approach that produces more equality.

Does Innovation Require Market Power?

Thus far, we have only distinguished between a successful and unsuccessful entrepreneur with the difference being the amount of wealth they appropriate after the fact. We have not, however, talked about how their innovation translates into that wealth. That requires you to sell a product in the market for more than it costs to make it. You can invent the best product ever, but if others can easily copy it, you will find that competition will drive the price of the product to cost, and eliminate any significant profits and hence wealth that you might have been otherwise able to earn.

The flip side of this notion is that if innovation is to have a monetary reward, innovators need to acquire some market power so they can charge as well as earn more. This is what patents, copyrights, and trade secrets are all designed for: to protect creative innovations from imitative competition. Alas, that means you pay higher prices.

The usual defense that is made here is that these transactions are voluntary. An entrepreneur cannot compel consumers to purchase their new products. For instance, former Council of Economic Advisers chair N. Gregory Mankiw writes,

> Then, one day, this egalitarian utopia [where everyone has the same wealth] is disturbed by an entrepreneur with an idea for a new product. Think of the entrepreneur as Steve Jobs as he develops the iPod, J.K. Rowling as she writes her Harry Potter books, or Steven Spielberg as he directs his blockbuster movies. When the entrepreneur's product is introduced, everyone in society wants to buy it. They each part with, say, $100. The transaction is a voluntary exchange, so it must make both the buyer and the seller better off. But because there are many buyers and only one seller, the distribution of economic well-being is now vastly unequal. The new product makes the entrepreneur much richer than everyone else.[22]

Mankiw is quite clear here. How can it be a bad thing if an entrepreneur chooses a high price and convinces some consumers to pay for it? This is, by definition, an improvement to social productivity as something new is being sold and people are buying it. Comparing the scenarios with and without an entrepreneur who has some market power, he argues that the world is better for it.

While Mankiw's argument is logical for what it is, we should ask if he is using the right comparison. Market power has a consequence, and that consequence is directly related to inequality. When a product is priced above its cost, then some people are excluded from purchasing it. If it is people who do not want to buy the product, that is one thing. But what if it is people who cannot afford the product even though they place great value on it? For an economist, there is no easy way to tell, so we generally favor lower prices. The lower price redistributes income from the entrepreneur to consumers who would have bought the product anyway, but it also allows those who would not have bought the product to buy it. Since the seller is still covering the product's cost, this is a social gain.

These trade-offs become stark when firms more aggressively exploit their market power. A case in point is Martin Shkreli, the founder and CEO of Turing Pharmaceuticals. This company looked for drugs that were actually out of patent yet had already been approved by the US Food and Drug Administration. Theoretically, they were subject to competition from generic drugs, but because it can be costly for those generics to reach the market, Turing Pharmaceuticals had market power. In 2015, Shkreli increased the price of AIDS drug Daraprim from $13.50 to $750 per pill. While some generic drug manufacturers eventually responded by producing equivalent products, Turing Pharmaceuticals was able to keep prices high for a significant period of time before competitive pressure to lower prices was felt. Shkreli is currently serving a seven-year sentence for securities fraud.

The regulations that led to this situation had been designed to promote innovation. But while the idea is to ensure that inventors can cover their research and development costs along with additional risk factors, the consequences can last for a long time. Daraprim was an old drug—approved by the Food and Drug Administration in 1953. The power that Turing Pharmaceuticals was able to wield arose because the United States prohibited imports of drugs—again, nominally to protect inventors. Not every country does this. In Australia, where Daraprim sells for eighteen cents a pill, a group of high schoolers was able to synthesize the drug. What this case shows is that given the uncertainties that arise from invention, having protections that last for more than half a century is unlikely to stimulate invention. The result instead is to protect the market power of the few at the expense of the many. By getting patent law right, we can have more innovation as well as equality.

While some market power is required to encourage entrepreneurship, the costs rise dramatically when there is too much or it is available for too long. The question is, How much would we be willing to pay so that entrepreneurs receive a reward? In a strict economic sense, this is a question of the price for outsourcing knowledge creation.

Nobel laureate Jean Tirole and his collaborator Glen Weyl tackle this question head-on. If you were outsourcing innovation to entrepreneurs, is it a good idea to reward them with market power as opposed to some fixed payment? Market power gives inventors an opportunity to directly deal with consumers while a fixed prize requires someone, in this case the government, to set the reward. Put in this way, the problem the government faces is that it does not know much about the nature of demand for innovative products. By contrast, granting entrepreneurs a monopoly means that their rewards are tied to that demand. Even a monopolist has to find a way for consumers to buy their products. In this regard, using a reward of market power provides a way of encouraging innovations that maximize the gap between the benefits and costs of innovations. The implication here is that if we outsource innovation to creative geniuses, we do it in a way that allows them to charge high prices.

At the core of this argument is not just the reward to innovation but also the signal markets can send about an innovation's value. What Weyl and Tirole argue is that when entrepreneurs have some monopoly power, they will consider not only how many people would be interested in buying their product but also in whether there are a few of them willing to pay a lot for it. If we were to regulate prices to reflect costs rather than demand, we would incentivize entrepreneurs to create mass-market products that are only a small improvement over existing ones. The products that were a major improvement, especially for a smaller group of people, would be avoided. By contrast, allowing the entrepreneur to price free of competitive forces aligns with their incentives to create products that are of the highest aggregate consumer value—even if these are concentrated in the hands of a few.

Arguments such as these imply that there is a difference between "taxation" via the prevention of higher prices and direct taxation of entrepreneurial incomes. So long as the direct tax paid is proportional to income, an entrepreneur with the market power to set their own high prices still has an incentive to pursue innovations that maximize their pretax profit and so receive appropriate market signals as to the types of innovations they pursue. In practice, things turn out to be a little more complicated, as many entrepreneurs have become adept at hiding intellectual property revenue from tax authorities.

The Risk Argument

Until this point, we have focused on the rewards people need in order to become entrepreneurs. Yet a person deciding to invent is only one input into an entrepreneurial venture. Critically, ventures often need capital to fund research, development, and commercialization. As entrepreneurship is risky, with a low probability of success, providers of capital to ventures will only invest if the return they expect is sufficiently high relative to the risk of failure.

The risk argument differs from the reward argument in that its basis is wealth inequality before rather than after the fact. Recall that the reward argument says that "after the fact" inequality arises because some entrepreneurs succeed and that is the reward for their earlier efforts. The risk argument does not suggest necessarily that "after the fact" inequality will arise among the winners and losers. Its point is that those who already have wealth will be more willing to take risks on their investments and support entrepreneurial ventures. Just as some Silicon Valley billionaires have gone on to become investors in new start-ups, the logic here is that a bit more inequality benefits society by facilitating more investment in moonshot companies. Put simply, if everyone in the United States had one extra cent, no one would be able to make any kind of meaningful investment. But if one lucky person had $3 million, that multimillionaire would be capable of investing in someone else's innovation.

The problem with this reasoning is that it is grounded in the premise of flawed financial markets. We can easily imagine a situation in which wealth was more equitably distributed, but financial markets created opportunities for households to pool their funds and support risky ventures. In that way, everyone's one cent contribution can add up to what is needed for the investment. Indeed, the whole point of having an efficient set of financial markets is that you do not need wealth concentration in order to provide socially beneficial finance to ventures and projects. But studies of credit rationing have shown that financial markets aren't always efficient when it comes to small business loans. Women, African Americans, Hispanics, and Asian Americans tend to be offered credit at higher interest rates, and are more likely to be denied a loan entirely.[23] Rather than letting inequality rip in the hope that it will boost the availability of start-up loans, wouldn't it be smarter to stamp out discrimination in financial markets?

A related argument, proposed by George Mason University's Tyler Cowen, is that inequality in the consumer market is a marker of an innovative society.[24] Suppose that the price of a new medical treatment roughly reflects its value to society. Cowen maintains that if everyone can afford all the available treatments, then it probably indicates that technology is advancing too slowly. By contrast, he contends, new advances like personalized medicine may well be out of financial reach for some people— but they provide evidence that health innovation is outpacing overall economic growth.

It's a provocative assertion, but not one that says that inequality is necessary to encourage inventions. Sure, kings had indoor toilets before peasants, but the massive wealth gap between royals and serfs didn't spur innovation. Cowen is right to say that the rich are the first to gain access to new inventions, yet that doesn't mean we need more inequality to boost entrepreneurship. Indeed, if past societies had been more equal, it might not have only been the affluent who could afford to flush their effluent.

Inequality Not Required

This chapter has asked, Do some people need to be richer than other people for innovation to occur? We looked at two factors. First, do people need to believe that any return they have as a result of innovation has to be untaxed in order to encourage them to innovate? Second, do holders of capital have to be rich in order to take the risk of funding innovation? To both questions, we answered "no."

The reason is simple. A world in which innovation was not rewarded would not be conducive to entrepreneurship. But requiring top earners to be shielded from taxation is not a necessary price to pay for that innovation. When closely examined, the argument for privileging the rich as a means of encouraging entrepreneurship starts to sound a little like one made by Ted Baxter, the bumbling news reader in the 1970s' sitcom *The Mary Tyler Moore Show*. When discussing the issue of overpopulation, Baxter proclaimed that he intended to have six children. Why? It would increase the chances that one of them would solve the population problem!

Being a successful entrepreneur requires several miracles to occur. The evidence suggests that more entrepreneurs can be created by reducing initial barriers and risks associated with becoming an entrepreneur. By contrast, changes in the magnitude of wealth that arises only when all the miracles have gone in one's favor matter relatively little.

If we want to encourage innovation, it doesn't make sense to let inequality rip. Starving the government of tax revenue will undermine public-sector innovation. We also need to ensure that the rewards from innovating are tied to those who bear the costs—in terms of labor or capital. Put simply, entrepreneurship is only one way that people acquire wealth. More common roads to riches include inheritance, luck, and land speculation. It would be both unfair and inefficient to benefit all top earners because we want to encourage more innovation. Merely increasing inequality will not do much to boost entrepreneurship and could well be counterproductive.

5 Does Innovation Cause Inequality?

Three tech giants—Google, Apple, and Facebook—are headquartered in the heart of Silicon Valley, an hour or two south of San Francisco. Silicon Valley is deep suburbia, and not surprisingly, isn't attractive to younger people with highly prized technical skills. So many programmers live in San Francisco or Oakland, and make a daily trek along Highways 101 or 280.

Given that technology workers were already putting in long hours, it did not take long for their employers to step up and make the commuting time productive. They established their own private bus system, with comfortable seats, Wi-Fi, and access to drinks. In the process, those buses became a symbol.

Writer Rebecca Solnit captured the mood, likening the buses to "spaceships on which our alien overlords have landed to rule over us."[1] She pointed to cultural icons and poets being pushed out of favored San Francisco neighborhoods. In 2014, buses carrying tech workers were blocked by angry locals. Protesters in Oakland threw rocks at the special buses.

The protesters were pointing the finger at the impact that Silicon Valley's most successful companies were having on rents in the Bay Area. That rents increase when regions prosper isn't new. But gleaming private buses run by the technology companies were like a finger in the eye to locals now struggling to pay the rent. Many San Francisco tenants would probably have foregone the access to the world's information that Google gave them in exchange for being able to pay 1990s rents again.[2]

What is happening to jobs is also happening to cities. In chapter 3, we discussed how technology is eliminating routine jobs and exacerbating wage inequality. But the same forces are also squeezing out affordable city homes, and making it harder for people on modest incomes to buy or rent in popular places. The average Manhattan apartment now rents for over $40,000 per year.[3] That amount is slightly above the average disposable income per person in the United States.[4] Gentrification is to cities as job destruction is to labor markets. As urban studies theorist Richard Florida pointed out, "Techies and tech startups are just the latest players in a much longer running battle over urban space."[5]

The tripling of San Francisco rents over the past generation has priced out many locals.[6] But other locals benefit from the influx of new arrivals. Old neighborhoods were upgraded. New buildings were created (the 1,070-foot Salesforce Tower opened in 2018). Restaurants and cafés are booming. A bike store owner in Oakland who used to literally watch tumbleweeds go by claimed, "Now I've got people walking in every few minutes."[7]

Seen in this way, the protests looked like familiar complaints about progress. This, in turn, spurred anger from the rich. The most extreme came in the form of a letter to the *Wall Street Journal* by billionaire Tom Perkins, who observed, "Writing from the epicenter of progressive thought, San Francisco, I would call attention to the parallels of fascist Nazi Germany to its war on its 'one percent,' namely its Jews, to the progressive war on the American one percent, namely the 'rich.' … This is a very dangerous drift in our American thinking. Kristallnacht was unthinkable in 1930; is its descendent 'progressive' radicalism unthinkable now?"[8] Perkins's response epitomized Godwin's law—the rule that once a debate goes on long enough, someone invariably mentions Adolf Hitler. But it also illustrated the widespread sense among the nation's tycoons that they were under attack.

One of the most vocal on this topic was Graham, who we heard about in the last chapter as a self-proclaimed "manufacturer of inequality." Following a successful entrepreneurial career, Graham had cofounded Y Combinator, the world's most successful start-up accelerator program. Each year, Y Combinator selects over a hundred (mostly) young entrepreneurs to put through a three-month program designed to turn their ideas into start-ups.[9] It offers funding (in return for an equity stake) and mentorship. Out of its program has emerged a network of thousands of entrepreneurs including Dropbox, Stripe, Reddit, Coinbase, Zenefits, Instacart, and Airbnb. Most are located in Silicon Valley.

This track record made Graham sensitive to arguments regarding how innovation in Silicon Valley might be generating inequality. As he puts it, "I've become an expert on how to increase economic inequality, and I've spent the past decade working hard to do it. Not just by helping the 2,400 founders Y Combinator has funded. I've also written essays encouraging people to increase economic inequality and giving them detailed instructions showing how."[10] Now it should not be surprising that if this is your view of yourself in the world, when you see people attacking economic inequality, you would tend to be defensive. And that is precisely what Graham proceeds to do: defend inequality.

He argues that his activities will make people rich, and if you want to stop that, then you will get less start-up activity and innovation. At first blush, this might seem to have a certain logic, but remember that people can get rich without increasing inequality. To take the simplest example, if a poor person enters Y Combinator and moves into the middle class, inequality falls. Even if that isn't happening, then it is possible that the entrepreneur's innovations may improve well-being more broadly. The social entrepreneurs who created GiveWell have helped direct billions of dollars of philanthropy into more effective charities, thereby reducing poverty across the globe. There is no iron law that says a start-up needs to benefit the rich more than the poor.

From airbags to vaccines, innovation has the potential to create jobs, expand choices, and improve the quality of life for everyone. Another benefit comes from process innovation, which has the potential to drive down prices—making technologies that were once accessible only to the superrich available to all. While there "ought" to be no trade-off, it is entirely possible that something is getting in the way and choking off the mechanisms by which everyone benefits.

Are Start-Ups Increasing Inequality?

Before turning to innovation in general and its impact on the economy, let's dig deeper into the particular type of innovation that occurs in Silicon Valley—start-up innovation. What we call "start-ups" are not simply new businesses. Instead, a defining feature of start-up businesses is that they are geared toward growth. Those businesses end up creating jobs, and can end up generating lots of wealth for their founders (and investors).

Start-ups do not arise uniformly across locations. The past half century has taught us that they tend to cluster together. MIT researchers Jorge Guzman and Scott Stern demonstrated this recently by developing a set of factors that could predict success among newly formed start-ups, including whether the firm was incorporated, whether it held some patents, and even the length of its name (start-ups with shorter names tend to perform better). Armed with that, Guzman and Stern could then look at businesses established more recently to project their growth potential. They did so and then mapped it. What they found is that Silicon Valley lit up like a Christmas tree. Other bright spots included Kendall Square in Cambridge, Massachusetts, and Silicon Beach in West Los Angeles. Moreover, for Silicon Valley, they did not find that all the recent start-up activity was in the traditional South Bay. Indeed, much of it was now located in San Francisco itself. Companies like Twitter had set up there, and employees who loved the Golden City could now walk to work.[11]

What this meant is that start-ups were more likely to be in some places than others. This also meant that economists could see whether inequality followed suit. The University of Toronto's Astrid Marinoni matched the location of high-growth start-ups in California with local measures of income inequality. Across the state, she found that places with more start-ups also have more inequality. The association was even stronger when looking at measures that considered commuting patterns.[12]

This is only the beginning of the story. It raises a puzzle. If entrepreneurial innovation is increasing inequality, what is getting in the way of broader benefits? Are there choke points that prevent everyone from sharing the spoils?

Choke Points

Trademark law has an odd quirk. New companies can register their names so that others can't use them. But if your company's name becomes so common that people start associating it with the whole product category, you can lose the trademark. One upon a time, kleenex, yo-yo, cellophane, aspirin, and escalator referred to specific products. They suffered "genericide," as courts stripped away their trademarks.

In 2017, a federal appeals court considered whether the same fate should befall Google. Pointing to a song in which rapper T-Pain says "Google my name," the plaintiffs argued that googling had become a generic term for internet search. Just as we might say "I'm going to take an aspirin" before popping an ibuprofen, the litigants suggested that people might say "I'll just google it" before plugging their search into Yahoo!

Although the court sided with Google, the case was a powerful illustration of the search engine's market dominance. In the United States, 88 percent of internet searches are done on Google.[13] The next closest rival, Bing has just 6 percent of the search market, followed by Yahoo! at 4 percent and DuckDuckGo at 1 percent.

As the internet grew, one of its features was supposed to be that it would reduce the barriers to starting a new firm. In the world of software, the argument went, anyone could start a company in their dorm room, garage, or basement. Unlike traditional brick-and-mortar businesses, you didn't have to be able to take out a loan for things such as brick and mortar. Viral marketing could take the place of expensive advertising campaigns. When switching could be done with the click of a button, brand loyalty might be a thing of the past.

Part of the problem is that there are massive returns to being the best. If you're a consumer choosing a free product, who wants to use the second-best social network, the second-best search engine, or the second-best shopping marketplace? In traditional industries, powerful firms sometimes amassed market share by making it hard for customers to switch. For firms such as Google and Amazon, it is the very ease with which customers can switch that has allowed them to dominate their industries.

Even where competitors can offer a lower price, they may still struggle to compete in markets where network effects matter. If you're buying a cell phone, there's an advantage in going with the company that has the largest coverage. If you're selecting a gaming console, you'll want one with plenty of great games.

For a brief period, start-ups demanded more technology workers than did established companies. From 1995 to 2001, the share of information-sector employees who worked for a start-up doubled. But after the tech crunch, it began to decline. The share of information technology workers at new firms is lower than at any time in the past generation.[14]

The same pattern holds when we look at all categories of workers—not just those in technology. Across the US economy, the share of people working at small, young firms is declining. In the early 1980s, 16 percent of workers were at firms that had been created in the previous five years. Three decades later, only 8 percent of workers were at young firms.[15] One study suggests that the increasing cost of starting a business is one factor that has pushed up wealth inequality over the past generation.[16]

Meanwhile, the pace of merger activity is accelerating. In the 1980s, US merger activity amounted to a few hundred billion dollars per year.[17] But in recent years, the average annual value of mergers has been around $2 trillion. We've seen computer firm Dell buy EMC, chemical firm Dow bid for DuPont, AT&T bid for Time Warner, and pharmaceutical giant Actavis buy Allergan. The minnows aren't spawning, and the whales are joining up in ever-larger pods.

At the Organisation for Economic Co-operation and Development (OECD), a team of researchers has noticed a divergence between high- and low-productivity firms.[18] Across advanced nations, they find that since the start of the century, "frontier firms" have enjoyed productivity growth of 3 to 4 percent annually, while "laggard firms" have experienced productivity growth around half a percent per year. The gap is particularly pronounced in sectors with large barriers to entry and in industries where "winner-takes-all" dynamics dominate competition. Those companies at the global productivity frontier are three to four times as productive as laggard firms. They are more likely to be part of a multinational group and tend to use more capital.

Within the United States, frontier firms are increasingly dominant. Analyzing the share of sales accounted for by the largest four firms, one study found that from 1982 to 2012, the market share of the largest four firms rose from 38 to 43 percent in manufacturing, from 11 to 15 percent in services, and from 15 to 30 percent in retail trade.[19] Research by *The Economist* concluded that since the 1990s, two-thirds of US industries have become more concentrated.

As the top firms have increased their market share, their profits have grown dramatically. In the 1960s and 1970s, the top tenth of firms earned an annual return on capital of around 20 percent. By the late 1990s, this had risen to 40 percent. Today, the top tenth of firms earn an annual return on capital of around 100 percent. These frontier firms are pulling away from the rest. In the 1990s, their return on capital was three times larger than the median firm. Now it's eight times larger.[20]

When economists see firms making an annual return on capital of 100 percent—and doing so persistently—we are inclined to think that the firm might be enjoying economic "rents." This doesn't mean they're moonlighting as landlords; it's a term that we use to describe profits that are above what would be needed to justify investments or efforts. It also is a significant clue as to where the value from new innovation is ending up.

Trickle Down?

One intriguing study by London Business School's Simcha Barkai looks at the evolution of profits in nonfinancial corporations over the past generation.[21] In the mid-1980s, profits were less than 5 percent of the gross value added. By the mid-2010s, profits had risen to over 15 percent. This increase in profits equates to over $1 trillion annually. Falling competition and rising markups have delivered a profit tsunami to US shareholders.

But wait, don't profits flow through to families? Or as Republican presidential hopeful Mitt Romney shouted to a heckler, "Corporations are people, my friend. … Everything corporations earn ultimately goes to people. Where do you think it goes?" Let's take a moment to explore what we might call "the Romney critique." To make things simple, we will ignore the fact that US corporations have foreign customers and foreign owners, focusing just on the domestic story.

If stock ownership and consumption were evenly distributed across the population, then rising profits would have minimal impact on inequality. People might frown at having to overpay for an airline ticket, but they'd soon start smiling when they realized that they held shares in the airline. Higher dividends and capital gains would largely compensate for higher prices.

It turns out, however, that the typical shareholder is a good deal better off than the typical consumer. The top fifth of the US population accounts for 39 percent of the consumption, but holds 89 percent of the shares.[22] By shifting money from consumers to shareholders, excess markups effectively channel resources from the poor to the rich. Market power might be one reason for the growth in inequality.

Where market power raises the "creation price," it might serve as a valuable incentive to innovate. But as the OECD has shown, market power often exists because of unreasonable barriers that stand in the way of new firms.[23] In other cases, consumers are paying higher prices because dominant firms are using their muscle to protect their position in the market.

Being big doesn't make you a bully, but it is hard to twist arms if you are scrawny. Companies with high market shares have a greater motivation and capacity to engage in anticompetitive conduct, such as predatory pricing, bid rigging, dividing territories, price fixing, and boycotting. A hint of this kind of misconduct comes from a study that attempts to figure out the extent of cartel conduct by using discovered cartels, which is a bit like calculating the volume of icebergs when you can only see the tops. On the assumption that authorities discover one in five cartels, this suggests that cartel commerce amounts to about $2 trillion annually. If cartels raise prices by 10 to 30 percent, the extra cost to consumers would be hundreds of billions of dollars each year.[24]

What about the impact of market concentration on workers? For the lucky few who work at frontier firms, there is some evidence that fatter profits have translated into healthier paychecks. While executives have done better than those on the shop floor, there does seem to be a firm-wide effect.[25] As one study sums up the result, "It's where you work."[26] In companies where managers earn more, janitors also tend to get higher wages.[27]

But it isn't enough to look at how the wage bill is divided up across the workforce. We also need to step back and consider the impact of market power on the total wage bill. One of the striking trends over the past generation has been the steady decline in the share of national income going to workers. In the 1970s, workers received around sixty-four cents out of every dollar of national income. By the 2010s, this had fallen to fifty-eight cents to the dollar.[28]

The falling labor share is a worldwide phenomenon. Over the past generation, the labor share has also fallen in China, Japan, Germany, Austria, Spain, and Australia.[29] Globally, the share of income going to employees has fallen by 4 to 6 percentage points since 1970.[30]

Underlying the fall in the labor share appears to be a rise in market concentration. Looking across industries, firms, and countries, Autor and coauthors document a clear pattern: where concentration goes up, the share of income going to workers goes down.[31] An increasing number of industries are "winner-take-most" sectors, in which one or two large players rule the roost. When this happens, the labor share tends to decline.

Technology is at the heart of these changes. Autor and colleagues demonstrate that industries that produce more patents (a common, though imperfect, measure of technical change) tend to have seen a larger increase in market concentration. They point out a number of different ways that these "superstar firms" have benefited from technological change.[32] As the internet has made price comparison easier, consumers tend to shift toward the cheapest product.[33] "Network effects" benefit firms that have strong online networks (think Facebook and Snapchat) or physical networks (think Uber and FedEx).

With cash-rich balance sheets, the biggest technology companies have been quick to buy potential rivals. Among Google's many acquisitions are Waze, YouTube, and Nest. Facebook has bought Instagram, Oculus VR, and WhatsApp. Amazon has acquired Audible, Zappos, and Whole Foods. The rapid pace of mergers has led some critics to ask whether antitrust law was right to move away from a structuralist approach and its focus on entry barriers. Driven by Chicago school economists in the late 1970s and early 1980s, this movement had a powerful influence on the federal government's merger guidelines and the US Supreme Court's interpretation of antitrust law.[34] In chapter 6, we discuss how competition policy might be usefully augmented to deal with the market power of the tech titans— delivering outcomes that are both more equitable and more efficient.

Is Ownership Really Diverse?

Another driver of rising market concentration is common ownership. Suppose that you and I each own companies that are duking it out for market share. You have an incentive to lure away my customers, and I have an incentive to lure away yours. Now suppose that we each own half of the two companies. In this case, there's a much weaker incentive to engage in a price war. Because we jointly own them, we'll both be better off if our two companies collude to drive up prices.

Alongside the increase in market concentration, there has been an increase in common ownership. Compared with a generation ago, shareholders are more likely to own multiple competing firms than just one. And again, technology has played a central role.

To see what's going on here, we need to take a brief detour into the world of stock market investing. In the past, almost all investors were persuaded by the arguments of active managers, who told them that the "smart" approach was to pay experts to pick the best portfolio of stocks. The lure of beating the market was seductive: Why settle for average?

Eventually, however, it became clear that most actively managed funds weren't beating the stock market. In fact, once their fat fees had been deducted, they were underperforming the stock index. Armed with this realization, economist John Bogle founded Vanguard in 1974, and started the first index fund the following year. Initially derided as "unAmerican," it was dubbed "Bogle's Folly." Attacking Vanguard, a competitor's flyer asked rhetorically, "Who wants to be operated on by an average surgeon, be advised by an average lawyer, or be an average registered representative, or do anything no better or worse than average?"[35]

It wasn't until the 1990s when index funds took off, rising over the course of the decade from 2 to 13 percent of the market.[36] In 2005, Nobel laureate Paul Samuelson ranked "this Bogle invention along with the invention of the wheel, the alphabet, [and] Gutenberg printing." Today, index investors account for more than one-third of the market. Even the world's most successful investor, Buffett, has written that "a low-cost fund is the most sensible equity investment for the great majority of investors."

The concept of buying the index is straightforward. You simply own a portfolio of shares that mirrors the stock exchange. So if Apple comprises 3 percent of the market, it will comprise 3 percent of your index fund. Computer trading algorithms ensure that index investments match the market. This simplicity means that investors end up flocking to the index fund with the lowest management fees. As a result, scale is critical in index investing. Once a firm has set up the infrastructure to run an index fund, the additional cost of investing another million dollars is almost zero. So the more money they attract, the smaller the percentage they need to charge in order to cover their costs. New index investment funds typically don't face explicit barriers to entry; their problem is that they just can't get their costs low enough to compete with the titans.

As a result, index funds are one of the most concentrated sectors in the United States. Between them, BlackRock, Vanguard, and State Street comprise 83 percent of the US market, and run the world's fifty-largest funds. As one analyst puts it, "It's basically a battle between King Kong, Godzilla, and Mothra, with everybody else fighting over scraps and crumbs."[37] Investors benefit from bargain-basement management fees, which would be a pure social gain if the rise of index fund behemoths didn't create other problems.

Which brings us back to common ownership.

For nine out of ten of the top five hundred firms in the United States, the trio of BlackRock, Vanguard, and State Street constitute the largest shareholder.[38] These firms may be fighting among themselves to attract customers into their index funds. But as shareholders, they have a powerful incentive not to encourage companies to fight to the death. Owning the index is a smart investment decision for most individuals to make. When you own the index, though, you have a stake in multiple competing companies. The impact on competition is akin to what might happen if sports fans jettisoned their favorite team and began barracking for all teams in the tournament, in proportion to their win-loss ratio. Collectively, low-cost index funds have acted to reduce the competitive pressures in the US economy.

Looking at the airline industry, one study finds that rising common ownership has increased prices by as much as one-tenth.[39] Another piece of research explores common ownership in the banking sector, and finds that its growth has led to customers paying higher fees and getting a lower return on their bank deposits.[40] The United States' largest banks—Bank of America, Citigroup, JPMorgan Chase, PNC Financial, US Bancorp, and Wells Fargo—all count among their five-largest shareholders the trio of BlackRock, Vanguard, and State Street. Sovereign wealth funds such as Norges Bank play a similar role.

Technology put a turbocharger under the hood of the world's biggest index funds. But in turn, those index funds risk becoming an anticompetitive force in the economy.

A Clearer Picture

Let's draw some of the threads together. Recent decades have seen an increasing divergence between frontier and laggard firms, with tech giants overrepresented on the frontier. Across a host of industries, the US economy has become more concentrated. This combination of higher profits and higher prices exacerbates inequality because those who own firms tend to be richer than their customers. Meanwhile, market concentration has squeezed down the share of income going to employees. Technology is at play in all kinds of subtle ways, from the monopolization of data by platform providers to control of ownership by index funds.

At an aggregate level, studies that look at the relationship between innovation and inequality find a clear connection. One set of researchers examine the relationship between innovation and top income inequality across states, using patent rates (which, as we have noted, are not a perfect measure of innovation). Their theoretical framework is based on Schumpeter's theory that the engine of capitalism is kept in motion by the "perennial gale of creative destruction"—a concept we discussed in chapter 1. Empirically, they find that states with more quality-adjusted patents tend to have higher inequality and higher social mobility, meaning more movement up and down the pecking order. From 1975 to 2010, they argue that increasing innovation can explain around one-fifth of the total increase in top income inequality. The relationship weakens in states where there appear to be entry barriers—suggesting that where new firms are locked out of markets, there is less inequality and less mobility.[41]

Other research looks across advanced countries, and finds that lowering the barriers to digital innovation has the effect of spurring both start-ups and superstars. OECD researchers Dominique Guellec and Caroline Paunov give the example of cloud computing, which has allowed technology firms to grow rapidly without the need to spend millions of dollars on mainframes and hard drives. Yet as they point out, the benefits of this kind of innovation do not necessarily accrue to customers. Instead, "they are mainly shared among shareholders and investors, top executives and key employees of the winning firms, who are already in the top tier of the income distribution (as they own capital and skills and hold managerial and leading positions in firms), hence contributing to increased income inequalities."

How might future technological changes affect these patterns? While economists do not have a perfect crystal ball, emerging technologies such as new energy supplies, advanced robotics, biotechnology, crowdsourcing, mobile internet, and big data have common features. First, they are likely to improve our quality of life. From smarter smartphones to life-extending drugs, technological advances have significant consumer benefits. Second, they will bring major changes to the labor market, from manufacturing workers displaced by 3-D printing to job creation in the solar panels installation industry. Third, they have the winner-take-most characteristics that make them ripe for domination by a handful of superstar firms. And fourth, they may serve as platforms that drive consolidation in nontechnology industries.

Economists often refer to "skill-biased technological change" as a driver of inequality. What we mean is that new innovations tend to advantage the haves more than the have-nots. In late eighteenth-century Britain, the steam engine was a greater boon to the wages of technically capable workers than unskilled laborers. Similarly, new innovations today are likely to be more advantageous to college graduates than to those who didn't finish high school. As frontier firms grow their market share, and common ownership dampens competitive pressures, there is a risk that large incumbents will snaffle most of the gains. New technology can worsen inequality, which in turn can create a backlash against innovation. To ensure the innovation engine keeps humming, it's vital to ensure that the fruits of growth are available to all. We return to this issue in chapter 7.

6 Encouraging Innovation

For most of human history, childbirth has been extremely dangerous. In evolutionary terms, mothers need a pelvis small enough to walk upright, while babies benefit from having bigger brains.[1] This makes childbirth a tight squeeze at the best of times. At worst, it can lead to fatal results. In 1817, Princess Charlotte of Wales, the heir to the English throne, died while giving birth. The child was stillborn, the king no longer had an heir, and so the throne passed to his brother and then niece, Victoria. The Victorian age was the product of a childbirth tragedy.

There were ways to potentially save both the mother and child in situations like this, but they were risky. Caesareans were generally safer for the child than the mother, who would have to endure the procedure without anesthetic. But perhaps the most significant innovation had been developed in London in the late fourteenth and early fifteenth century: forceps.

Forceps were actually two innovations that together made something useful. First, it was an instrument—the forceps themselves. These were basically tong-like objects designed to grasp a baby's head, designed to be pulled or guided out, depending on how you wanted to describe it. The second was the technique. It was the set of skills you would use to bring the baby out. Both are still used today, though at a diminishing rate. Medical writer and surgeon Atul Gawande laments that these sorts of skills are being lost as caesarean section procedures become more common. "We are seeing the waning of the art of childbirth. The skill required to bring a child in trouble safely through a vaginal delivery, however unevenly distributed, has been nurtured over centuries. In the medical mainstream, it will soon be lost."[2]

For a couple of centuries after the technique was invented, forceps delivery was an unknown practice. Peter Chamberlen and his descendants kept forceps a family secret. They went so far as to cover the lower portion of their patient during the procedure so no one could observe their "magic." Hugh Chamberlen, part of the third generation, tried to sell the technique to the French government, but he received some "bad press" regarding a failed delivery and so that transaction did not eventuate.[3] In the end, others did eventually work out the technique, although each had an incentive to keep the knowledge to themselves. By the mid-eighteenth century, the secret was out, but the skills were still not widespread enough to save Princess Charlotte.

The story of secrecy surrounding forceps illustrates two themes that are crucial when thinking about innovation. The first is that if you keep new knowledge secret, you necessarily prevent it from being used widely. So you may have an innovation, but its value to society is muted. The second is that by keeping a secret, you prevent others from innovating on top of it. Only the Chamberlen family had the opportunity to hone their technique. Had forceps been available and practiced widely, it is likely others would have had insights that would have improved the tool and the way it was used. Secrecy prevents use and future innovation itself.

A Patent for Your Thoughts?

It is worthwhile taking a moment to consider why it was that the Chamberlen family went to such lengths to control their invention. When it comes to commanding a price for something, there is nothing more valuable than when that something can save a life. Given the opportunity of paying for a lifesaving innovation or going without, people tend to be willing to hand over almost everything. This suggests that the Chamberlens wanted to be able to comfortably extract the wealth of the richest in society. But in fact that strategy—which they ended up pursuing—was setting their sights somewhat low.

Suppose that the Chamberlens had just been granted a twenty-year patent on their invention and came to ask you for advice on what they might do. You might advise them to license the device and training to obstetricians. Or to set up a franchise system in which forceps-trained obstetricians were spread out across the globe. Or to create a multinational company that performed forceps deliveries. In other words, the modern economist in us sees a failure to scale-up.

But none of this was possible in the late fourteenth and early fifteenth centuries. Without intellectual property protection, the Chamberlens feared that others would steal their invention and expertise. Global companies and international franchise networks were unknown at the time—and even if they had been known, the risk of intellectual theft would have rendered them untenable. Secrecy was the norm, and the Chamberlens were not the only medical innovators to practice it.[4]

The modern-day institution that most clearly counters secrecy is the patent system. Patents give their holders an exclusive right to commercialize their innovations—critically, to prevent others from doing it. In return for this property right, the patent holder has to tell the world precisely what they have invented. Such disclosures are useful. It is often the case that multiple people are thinking of the same idea, but only one has a breakthrough. When that happens, it is useful to tell others so they can turn their attention to the next challenge.

But the power of the patent comes from the protection it affords. It makes innovators less nervous about what others see of their ideas. If the Chamberlens had been armed with a patent, they would have been less worried about others stealing their invention. If were granted a twenty-year patent in 1500, they would have enjoyed stupendous wealth for twenty years. Then, from 1520 onward, anyone would have been free to make their own forceps, following the plans lodged with the Chamberlens' patent application. This outcome would have been more efficient (since more infant lives would have been saved) and more equitable (since those who gained access to the technology would have been poorer families).

In other settings, patents give entrepreneurs who may not have everything they need to commercialize an innovation the means of being able to sell it to others who do. Back in the 1960s, Bob Kearns was an engineer working and lecturing in Detroit. Due to an unfortunate wedding night accident involving a champagne cork, he was legally blind in his left eye.[5] When driving in a Michigan rainstorm, Kearns lamented the inability of his wipers to help him see better. In those days, windshield wipers had two settings—fast and slow—and they were always moving. Kearns's notion was that it should be possible to have a slower setting, in which the wipers paused briefly between each wipe.

Motivated by his own experience, as well as a long-standing desire to work for a big car company like Ford, Kearns spent years working out a way to make wipers pause. His solution relied on electronics—an unusual and innovative thing in those days. He fitted the mechanism to his own Ford Galaxie with most of the contraption inside a black box and drove it down to Ford to show its engineers. They pored over the car and were impressed. Kearns was then given the details of tests he would need to perform to become a Ford supplier. Those took months of work that Kearns completed in his basement. Ford, however, passed on him being a supplier, though the firm did employ Kearns for a brief period. In the meantime, Kearns filed for a patent on his invention.

It took seven years for Ford to work out Kearns's mechanism. Kearns discovered this when he saw an intermittent wiper in a new Ford model at a trade show. It was his invention. He sued the car giant.

Today, this might have been an easier case, but back in the 1970s, patents in the United States were not as strong. In addition, Ford itself was a tough litigant. Henry Ford had many years of struggles when a lawyer patented the automobile, and so his company had a culture resistant to patent litigation. Kearns became obsessed with the case, ruining his marriage, and prompting his children to become lawyers to help with his cause. It took twenty years, but Kearns eventually won a $10 million judgment from Ford. By then, every carmaker had put Kearns's mechanism in their vehicles. Eventually, Kearns won a $30 million judgment from Chrysler, but his cases against other automakers were dismissed on legal technicalities.

You might think that it all worked out. But Kearns lost a lifetime of inventing, and society lost what his inventive genius could have brought. Unless you are Elon Musk, you are not going to be able to invent something for the car industry and become a carmaker to bring it to market. The best you might hope for, as Kearns did, is to become a supplier. Yet in doing so, you face a risk: if all you have is an idea, then you are vulnerable to expropriation. Once you give up the secret, the idea can be copied, and then the only protection you have is that afforded by patent law. Indeed, subsequent research has shown that inventors are keenly aware of this.[6] When inventing something that fits into a larger picture that is controlled by others, they are much more likely to go ahead if they have secure intellectual property protection. Moreover, those who have such protection end up doing the deals with others; something that, for most ideas, is what allows them to come to market rather than languish.

Owning Your Ideas

This illustrates the point of the patent system: it is designed to make markets for ideas safe.[7] This is crucial in terms freedom to innovate, especially when inventors have little power. But just because an idea is patentable, it doesn't mean it is valuable. Take, for example, the patent for a dog watch: a watch a dog can wear, but that keeps "dog time"—human time multiplied by seven.[8] Since the dog watch patent expired eight years ago—or fifty-six years ago in dog time—the world has not been flooded by dog watches. The same goes for registered patents on a motorized ice cream cone, a forehead rest for urinals, a tricycle lawnmower, an anti-eating mouth cage, and a glass that administers electric shocks to cure hiccups. A patent is not an endorsement.

Bobby Edwards's mother, Judy, had a constipation problem. And it was getting worse as she got older. Then a doctor recommended that she use a footstool to raise her knees, and it worked. As it turns out, with your feet on the ground, your rectum is kinked and not free. This pressure can put unnecessary strain on other vital organs (Elvis Presley's fatal heart attack occurred while he was sitting on the toilet). But just using a regular footstool was awkward. Bobby Edwards saw an opportunity. What if the footstool was designed for the toilet with a groove to allow feet to be placed on the side rather than in front? There was nothing like it before, and so Squatty Potty was born in 2011 and patented in 2012.

The patent was necessary. Once designed, the Squatty Potty was just a bit of plastic. But even with that, to build a business it had to be marketed. That required innovation in and of itself, but Edwards used a video to explain the concept in an entertaining way with unicorns and colorful ice cream instead of poo. The video went viral and has been viewed a hundred million times. In 2016, Squatty Potty sales exceeded $30 million.[9]

The journey from having an idea on the toilet to building a business exhibits precisely what we want from the patent system. Without patent protection, cheap imitations would quickly have taken over. Edwards's patent gave him two decades to build and then profit from the market he had created. It made it safe for him to spend time and money refining the invention.

Innovation is hard. Before products are launched, there is much uncertainty as to their value. Afterward, however, what was initially strange can become mainstream (or not, as in the case of the Segway). From nonstick frying pans to touch screen computers, ideas that once seemed radical have become commonplace.

Not all innovation requires intellectual property protection. New York University's Petra Moser gives the example of the Netherlands and Switzerland in the late nineteenth century. These countries didn't enforce patents, but both produced a plethora of new innovations that featured at the world's fairs. Dutch and Swiss inventors did especially well at food-processing novelties. Milk chocolate, baby food, and ready-made soups were all invented in environments that provided no patent protection.[10] By keeping their recipes secret, food innovators were able to profit from their discoveries.

As George Mason University's Alexander Tabarrok points out, fashion, food, and sporting performance are among the industries where new ideas proliferate in the absence of copyright and patent protection.[11] This is because there are other ways (such as brands and reputation) of protecting ideas.

Secrecy rather than patents protects some of the world's most famous creations. The ingredients in Coca-Cola and formula for WD-40 are protected by secrecy. The recipe for Colonel Sanders's "11 secret herbs and spices" is locked in a vault in KFC's Louisville headquarters. Google's algorithm is kept confidential to prevent unscrupulous people from manipulating search rankings. If firms used patents to protect all their innovations, devious rivals would have little need to engage in cyberhacking; instead, they would simply go to the patent office.

Some inventions are not protected from copying at all. The open-source approach has helped create one of the world's most widely used computer operating systems (Linux), the largest-ever genetic maps (the Genographic Project), breakthroughs in astronomy (via NASA's photo-organizing project), and the world's largest encyclopedia (Wikipedia). In some sense, open source—which aims to increase take-up by offering services at a zero price—is the opposite of a monopoly—which charges a higher price and ends up serving fewer customers. Individuals who contribute to open-source projects gain the satisfaction of helping others and the kudos that comes from improving a service used by millions of others. Some companies support open-source projects in order to attract staff and customers, and because they can then charge for related services, such as training or certification.

Innovation flourishes when people can pursue their ideas without having them stolen by others. Big companies frequently have this ability by default. Smaller innovators need a government institution to help.

Something So Right, It's Wrong

As with anything like this, however, it can go too far. The same is true of intellectual property rights. We already talked about Martin Shkreli who used a patent on a pharmaceutical drug to move from low to "wealth-extracting" prices. If you happen to own the patent on something that is valuable when no one else can make the same product, the patent explicitly allows you to charge a monopoly price. The better question to ask is: why can that monopoly price be so high?

The dark side of intellectual property protection is when its reach is extended beyond what was intended. A patent is intended to be an exclusionary right that is temporary. In most countries, it lasts about 20 years from the date you file for a patent. By contrast, its sibling copyright has a much longer life, extending up to seventy years after the death of its creator. This means that if Beyoncé Knowles-Carter lives until age ninety, then her song "Bootylicious," which she cowrote in 2001 at age twenty, would be in copyright protection until 2141. A right that lasts for 140 years can hardly be called temporary.

The temporary nature of patent protection is important. First, it creates an incentive for the innovator to do something quickly to get the product out to market. The longer they wait, the less time they will have the market to themselves. Remember, the goal is to get the innovation out there—both by not being a secret but also as something that people can use. The second reason for temporariness is that once the patent runs out, people who want to use it in the market, or critically, innovate and build on top of it, no longer need to ask for the permission of the original inventor.

It is worth exploring this second notion more carefully. When Thomas Edison patented the incandescent light bulb, he succeeded in blocking competitors who offered products that in fact improved on his original design. The Wright brothers patented their aircraft design and became so litigious that one of their rivals joked that a person jumping in the air and waving their arms would get sued. Not surprisingly, the Wrights were more successful in blocking follow-on innovation in US courts than in France or

Germany. The Wrights' focus on litigation over innovation has been cited as the reason why European aviation was far in advance of US aviation innovation by the time World War I started. Only when the US government intervened were the patent issues resolved with US manufacturers pooling their patents and licensing to each other. But had the standoff persisted, it would have resolved itself with the expiration of both sets of patents (which at the time lasted for seventeen years).

Even Guglielmo Marconi, who patented the diode as part of his invention of the radio, refused to grant a license to AT&T, which invented the superior triode that infringed on his original patent. In each of these cases, improvements were delayed because the permission of the original innovator was required.[12] Why they didn't give such permission was strange as, in some cases, it may have been mutually profitable. Yet each of these cases illustrates why it is both equitable and efficient to grant patents for only a limited time.

What happens if an inventor can use their original patent to leverage their monopoly position beyond its term limit and scope? Qualcomm was responsible for an important invention at the heart of the cell phone industry. Prior to its invention, if you wanted to make a cell phone call, only one connection could be used at a time at a particular tower. This meant that carriers had to do little tricks—chunking your call into millisecond bursts—to make it seem like you weren't actually sharing. Taking turns to speak only worked if there weren't too many calls being made. Qualcomm's founder, Irwin Jacobs, changed all that with a new protocol—code division multiple access (CDMA)—that allowed calls to happen at the same time. Your phone was then responsible for putting together the right bits from a stream of data coming to it. The effect was like a directional microphone in a noisy room. The CDMA patent was applied for in 1990 (and granted in 1992). Qualcomm used it for its own products (in the form of chips) and also licensed it to others.

Fast-forward to today and Qualcomm is no longer a start-up like Squatty Potty with a clever idea protected by a patent. It is now a large company with 130,000 patents that are commemorated on a patent wall in the lobby of Qualcomm's headquarters. That original patent is long expired, but Qualcomm was able to continue innovating, and managed to build out patents to cover the improvements in spectrum use that we call 3G, 4G, and LTE today. That means that a chunk of the payments you make when you buy a cell phone still goes to Qualcomm. For a typical iPhone, it could easily be twenty dollars.

Qualcomm now finds itself under pressure for overextending its reach. Until 2018, it refused to license standard smartphone patents to competing chipmakers such as Intel. Qualcomm would only license them to firms that made smartphones, and then only if those firms bought Qualcomm chips. But in November 2018, the federal court ruled that Qualcomm had to license its patents to competing chipmakers.[13] Other court cases against Qualcomm, brought by the Federal Trade Commission, are still before the courts.

In perhaps the most public tussle, smartphone makers Apple and Samsung sued Qualcomm for overreach. Samsung successfully lobbied the South Korean government to scale back Qualcomm's claims. In Apple's case, it has other chip options than Qualcomm and wants to get a better deal. As it happens now, when Apple sells an iPhone XS with 256 GB for $1,149, it pays Qualcomm $5 more for its chip than for the same phone with just 64 GB of memory, which costs $999. This is despite the fact that Qualcomm's chip and patents have nothing to do with memory size. Apple argued that it should pay Qualcomm based on the price of the chip rather than the phone. The stakes were high. An Apple loss could have meant a ban on iPhone imports to the United States. Ultimately, Apple settled for around $4.5 billion.[14]

Legal arguments between large corporations aside, there is a fundamental philosophical issue at the heart of this debate. Some people contend that a company like Qualcomm should be able to leverage its original patent by any means it can (perhaps even to violate otherwise-standard antitrust laws). The logic is that the return it receives from leveraging its patent comes from its original research and so should be part of its reward. The counterargument is that if you can leverage your initial patent to future control of an industry, that means that everyone in the industry has to come to you for permission, and that limits the possibility for future innovation.

In the end, this might seem like a simple trade-off between the returns to inventive effort and the potential for seeing inventions used widely and cheaply. It is mitigated, however, by fundamental uncertainty. When Qualcomm was working toward CDMA in the 1980s, there was considerable uncertainty regarding where the industry would lead. Maybe Qualcomm would claim that it saw smartphones in the future. But even so, any rational basis for decision making suggests that the returns from this could not have added much to its cost-benefit analysis. This is precisely why patents are made to give exclusivity soon after invention rather than into the future. For any profit-minded entrepreneur, the near term is what drives decision making. Again, the efficient approach is also more equitable because it allows the benefits from a particular invention to be spread more widely.

All this discussion of patents focuses on the returns to innovators over a twenty-year horizon. Yet what about innovations that take many decades to pan out? Our point is not that long-term inventions are unimportant. They are. But it is not within the scope of the patent system or lax anti-trust laws to protect those kinds of inventions. Regardless of the strength of property rights, profits two decades away have minimal impact on decisions today. No patent should last longer than twenty years.

Indeed, some have even argued that intellectual property law could take a more nuanced approach than granting all patents for twenty years, irrespective of sector or complexity.[15] One proposal is to offer inventors a choice between shorter patents (which are easier to apply for) and longer ones (which require a higher standard of proof). We will return to this idea at the end of the chapter.

Permissionless Innovation

Because invention is inherently uncertain, society wants to minimize the roadblocks that we put in the way of innovators. Intellectual property law aside, some new innovations face problems due to outdated bylaws, risk-averse company cultures, and regulatory processes that focus only on the potential downsides. The more people you have to persuade, the more forms you have to fill out, the harder innovation becomes. As rear admiral Grace Hopper famously put it, "It's easier to ask forgiveness than it is to get permission." In his book *Permissionless Innovation*, George Mason University's Adam Thierer refers to this as "Hopper's law." The notion of permissionless innovation has become one of the core ideas that economists use to think about promoting innovation.[16]

Underpinning the notion of permissionless innovation is the principle that innovation should be judged innocent until proven guilty. Since encouraging experimentation has significant social value, the regulation of new ideas should move carefully. Laws that stymie new innovation should be based on evidence of concrete harm, not speculation about the worst-case scenario. Rules that create frictions can have large effects. Researchers found that when Norway created a friction on innovation—abandoning the "professor's privilege" that allowed university researchers to commercialize ideas without permission from their institution—commercialization rates fell by 50 percent.[17] Permissionless innovation bolsters the idea of a "regulatory sandbox" in which new financial technology innovations are given temporary permission to operate on a small scale.

A favorite question we ask students is: when do you think the answering machine was invented? Most remember that 1990s sitcoms such as *Seinfeld* had answering machines as part of the plot so they think it was in the 1970s or 1980s. In fact, it was 1934.[18] The answering machine was invented by AT&T, which at the time had a monopoly over US telephone services.

It was under AT&T's research arm that Clarence Hickman showed how to use magnetic recording technology to record a phone call. The technology operated just like the answering machines that appeared half a century later. It answered the call with a message and then allowed the caller to leave their own message to be played back later. When the caller hung up, the machine would disconnect.

Despite all this, AT&T did not produce anything like an answering machine until the 1950s. This was despite continual customer requests for the product. This seems surprising. The missed call is as old as the call itself. For several decades, though, AT&T executives not only suppressed their own use of magnetic recordings with regard to telephones but also actively blocked others from trying to do the same. They did not want calls recorded.

Why not? The answer was a fear and a theory. They feared that if people knew calls could be recorded, they would be reluctant to make them. And what is better evidence that calls can be recorded than an answering machine? As one manager wrote, "If at any time there was a reasonable probability that such a device [i.e., a magnetic recorder] was connected at one end or the other, it would change the whole nature of telephone conversations and would in our opinion render the telephone much less satisfactory and useful in the vast majority of cases in which it is employed. It would greatly restrict the use of the telephone."[19] This is an age-old fear: privacy. If people are worried that their conversations will not be private, they might not talk at all. The AT&T executives had no proof that their concerns were founded; that is part of the uncertainty that can surround innovations. But they were happy enough with their monopoly, which endured until antitrust regulators split the company into seven "Baby Bells" in 1982. When you're the dominant player in a multibillion-dollar market, why experiment with a new invention that might undermine people's comfort with telephones?

We know now that these fears were overstated. When answering machines became available, people adopted them without losing confidence in the telephone system. But because AT&T worried about the recording of calls, it moved to suppress its own extensive innovations in magnetic sound recording. The applications of that technology extended well beyond answering machines. Ultimately, German researchers commercialized magnetic recording and came to dominate the industry. The intrepid AT&T research team that built magnetic recording did not have permission to take its invention beyond the company's walls. Concentration has its downsides.

Opening the Networks

Ultimately, permission is most likely to present a barrier for innovation when the gatekeeper also has market power. If they don't face entities with market power, would-be innovators can choose from among a range of possible commercial partners. If a single monopolist controls the route to market, innovation may be trickier. The recent moves on "net neutrality" by US states can be thought of as about the "permission" for a content provider to have their traffic sent at the same speed as the large incumbents. If an internet service provider can cause its customers to pay different prices based on the content they supply, then content providers are vulnerable when setting up internet businesses. By outlawing such differential prices, net neutrality allows internet entrepreneurs to build businesses free of potential blocking tactics.[20]

This issue is, however, pervasive when it comes to industries that are dominated by firms with network effects—that is, where the value of a product to each user increases as the number of users rise. Take, for example, social media. Facebook and other platforms are insulated from competition because they have powerful network effects. There is nothing necessarily wrong with that from an antitrust perspective—it is a way that a monopoly can arise through ordinary activities and investments—but from a competition policy perspective, it means that it is difficult for competitors to come in and compete with Facebook.

This same issue arose in telecommunications competition. Back in the 1980s, it became obvious that if you wanted to deregulate telecommunications—moving away from a system in which carriers had a complete monopoly—you need to allow calls to be made and received across networks. That is, you needed interconnection between different telecommunications networks so they could effectively compete. For social media, the same principle applies. You want people to be able to communicate across networks. This would then mean that if someone were to invent a "better Facebook," they could connect their network to Facebook. Letting new social media platforms compete for individual Facebook users—rather than having to compete for the entire network—would encourage more competition among social media platforms, leading to better outcomes for users.

The insight is to understand that social media is just messages—they are richer than voice in some circumstances, have structure (in terms of likes and comments), and can often be broadcast rather than communicated one to one. The critical point is that it should not matter which network you are on; you should be able to engage with those to whom you have given permission.

One solution to this is to allow individuals to port their identity to other networks.[21] With that identity comes a set of permissions associated with it, and it is that which creates value here. A competitor to Facebook—call it, for the sake of argument, NoRussiaBook—could come in offer a different ad policy, and you could become a user. Your friends and connections need not know the difference—although we suspect transparency would be preferable. The resulting privacy issues are complicated, but that is largely because privacy itself is complicated, not because there is anything intolerably risky about identity portability per se.[22]

Such moves are not unprecedented. Governments (e.g., Estonia and India) and private organizations (e.g., Microsoft with Mastercard, IBM with Visa) are working to provide individuals with a digital identity. Identity portability faces technical challenges. Nonetheless, this type of creative approach is required if we are serious about encouraging competition in the digital space. There are several start-ups moving to solve this type of problem using blockchain technologies. Indeed, Facebook has solved this internally for two billion people. If Facebook were proactive, they could roll out identity portability and social network interoperability ahead of any regulation.

Other solutions—such as, breaking up Facebook by separating out Whats-App or Instagram—do nothing to resolve the underlying issue: network effects become barriers to entry. To encourage freer innovation, society needs to change the structure of the industry just as we did with telecommunications in the 1990s. This is another example of where aiming toward permissionless innovation systems generates more opportunity for competition (by lowering entry barriers) as well as providing avenues so that ingenious creators are not hemmed in by the power of the dominant industry players.

Government as Innovator

Until this point, we have implicitly assumed that innovation is a private-sector activity. Yet the history of technological breakthroughs shows that this is a long way from the truth. In World War II, government researchers produced radar, jet engines, and superglue (along with less socially useful technologies, such as assault rifles, cruise missiles, and the atomic bomb). NASA's Technology Transfer Program claims to have invented nearly two thousand spin-off products, including freeze-dried food, racing swimsuits, memory foam, and the DustBuster. Mariana Mazzucato of University College London points out that many of the technologies that make smartphones so smart came from government research programs, including voice recognition, global positioning systems, multitouch screens, lithium-ion batteries, the internet, and cellular technology.[23]

Government grants—such as those provided through the National Institutes of Health and the National Science Foundation—are another vital way in which the public sector spurs innovation. A recent study looked at the 210 new pharmaceuticals approved by the Food and Drug Administration over a seven-year period, aiming to discover how many had been supported by funding from the National Institutes of Health.[24] The answer: all of them. One hundred percent of the new drugs approved in this period benefited from government-supported research.

"Every major technological change in recent years," contends Mazzucato, "traces most of its funding back to the state." Moreover, she argues, such public investments were not riskless. "We pretend that the government was at best just in the background creating the basic conditions (skills, infrastructure, basic science). But the truth is that the involvement required massive risk taking along the entire innovation chain: basic research, applied research and early stage financing of companies themselves."[25]

As Fred Block of the University of California at Davis observes, the narrative of plucky entrepreneurs creating all the big ideas is fundamentally at odds with reality.[26] "The key inventions of the past two hundred years cannot be attributed to ingenious tinkering by inspired engineers or concerted initiatives by corporate laboratories," he writes.[27] Yet humans are storytelling creatures, so we are naturally drawn to accounts of the "eureka" moment when a brilliant entrepreneur arrived at a sudden breakthrough. This can lead us to miss the role of government and overstate the role of great people.

Naturally, research-funding bodies do not have a perfect crystal ball. That's why it is useful to have grants allocated by multiple organizations so as to encourage healthy competition between them. It is vital that foundations and institutes continue to take a risk on improbable ideas with potentially huge payoffs. A monopoly funder can become lazy and conservative—supporting only predictable, incremental research by teams with a proven track record. Multiple bodies can keep one another on their toes, taking more chances in a quest to find the next massive breakthrough.

Reducing the cost of entrepreneurship can stimulate more of it. One study found that the historical rollout of highways in the United States stimulated regional innovation.[28] The researchers argue that it was a reduction in the cost of knowledge flows that drove the improvement. Following the government's decision to deregulate the airline market, economists examined the impact of new direct flights on entrepreneurial firms.[29] They found that new routes increased both successful innovation and the likelihood of a successful exit by firms funded by venture capital. The idea here was that new direct airline routes reduced the costs of venture capital firms being matched with entrepreneurs. The boost to funding led to more entrepreneurship and innovation.

Specific educational programs that are designed to mentor, fund, and train undergraduate entrepreneurs have been found to have positive impacts, whether government supported or not. Economists studied the Next 36 entrepreneurship program in North America that gave undergraduates access to seed capital, mentorship, and intensive business education.[30] They found that for women and minorities, the program led to a 20 percent increase in the likelihood that they would subsequently be involved in an ongoing entrepreneurial venture.

The role of government in innovation has direct implications for the right level of taxation. As the late University of Chicago economist Milton Friedman reminded us, to tax is to spend.[31] If we cut taxes in an attempt to encourage more innovation, it may mean cutting spending on education and research. The result could be a less innovative society.

Lost Curies

It's one thing not to have to ask permission to run your own race. But that isn't much help if you can't even get to the starting line. A bright young entrepreneur in an affluent household can typically borrow money from their parents. They can draw on broad social networks to connect to suppliers, business partners, and customers. If they need to travel or study, they can count on family support.

By contrast, an equally bright entrepreneur in a poor family might lack access to loans and family networks. They may have a great idea, but struggle to find the resources to commercialize it. To such a person, talk of permissionless innovation might remind them of French writer Anatole France's riff on equal justice: "The law, in its majestic equality, forbids the rich as well as the poor to sleep under bridges, to beg in the streets, and to steal bread."[32]

A number of recent studies point to the disparity in inventing rates across society. Matching up millions of records, researchers are able to look at the family income of patent holders and compare this with the population at large. Again, patenting isn't a perfect measure of inventiveness, but it does tell us something useful about who gets an opportunity to innovate.

In Finland, children of parents in the top 1 percent of the income distribution are four times as likely to become an inventor as children whose parents are in the bottom half of the income distribution.[33] In the United States, the relationship between parental income and innovation is stronger still, with those who were born into the top 1 percent being nine times as likely to become inventors as those born into the bottom half of the income distribution.[34] Not only is this a stronger effect than in Finland, it is stronger than in the historical United States. In the late 1800s and early 1900s, children born into the top 1 percent were "only" about six times as likely to become inventors as those born into the bottom half of society.[35]

Delving deeper into the channels through which family background shapes entrepreneurship, another striking difference emerges. In Finland, the relationship between inventiveness and parental income is almost entirely explained by differences in standardized test scores. Among US inventors from a century ago, the relationship between patenting and family background is entirely explained by how many years of education the child receives.

But in today's United States, the relationship between inventiveness and family background does not disappear even when the researchers hold constant elementary school test scores or college quality. It is certainly true that students who have higher test scores or attend more selective colleges are more likely to lodge patents. But if we take two students who scored 90 percent on the same test, then the one with the higher parental income is more likely to become an inventor. The same is true at a college level. If you take two MIT students, the one with richer parents is more likely to lodge a patent.

A clue as to precisely how family background matters can be seen when the researchers look at some of the fine-grained patterns. Children who grow up in neighborhoods with a high rate of innovation in a particular industry are themselves more likely to lodge a patent in that industry. For example, a child who grows up in Minneapolis is particularly likely to patent a medical device, while a child from Silicon Valley is especially likely to lodge a computing patent. Parents matter too. If your mother or father lodged a patent in a specific field, such as modulators, then you are more likely to lodge a patent in precisely that field rather than a similar one such as oscillators.

It's easy to forget the role that such exposure plays in success. In 1968, parents in Seattle's elite Lakeside School took $3,000 from their rummage sale and bought a computer with a direct link to a mainframe machine in downtown Seattle. Consequently, a young Bill Gates and future Microsoft cofounder Paul Allen had an opportunity to program computers in real time. As writer Malcolm Gladwell notes, while most college students in that era were programming using punch cards, "Bill Gates got to do real-time programming as an eighth grader in 1968."[36] No one doubts Gates's brilliance, but his achievements owe a great deal to the extraordinary opportunities he received as a teenager.

Summing up their findings about the impact of family background on patenting in today's United States, one team of economists concluded that there are many "lost Einsteins" across the United States—"individuals who do not pursue a career in innovation even though they would have had highly impactful innovations had they done so."[37] We also emphasize the "lost Curies" here, since women are even more likely than men to miss out.[38] Creating opportunities for poor children, minorities, and girls to come into contact with innovators is likely to benefit not just those people but also likely to produce more inventions and higher productivity.

Lost Rembrandts

One way of looking at how new knowledge impacts the economy is that science produces fundamental knowledge that is the input to technology. In general, science comes out of academic institutions while technology is commercialized by business.

Interestingly, science is more geographically spread out than technology. Scientific research is concentrated in universities, which are dotted across the United States.[39] By contrast, US technology commercialization agglomerates in a handful of areas, including Silicon Valley, Boston, Seattle, New York, Austin, Los Angeles and Washington DC.[40] If you mapped them in profile, science would be like the rolling hills of Kentucky, and technology would be like the jagged peaks of Colorado.

Why is the distribution of scientific and technological talent so mismatched? While both require scientific talent, technology commercialization necessitates a particular type of business talent: judgment—specifically, being able to sort out what to do from what not to do. For science, going down fruitless paths is part of the process. For technology, it is decidedly unwelcome and potentially destructive. A researcher who picks too many fruitless paths takes longer to get tenure. A firm that picks too many fruitless paths goes bust.

In effect, there is a missing market for "judgment," which leads to much scientific research not even reaching commercial status. Without judgment, there is only so much that Silicon Valley can do. The result is akin to thousands of lost Rembrandt paintings gathering dust in attics.[41]

What is a market for judgment? It is, basically, the nexus between science and technology. A typical scientist with a new invention has deep technical knowledge but often no business experience. The same is true for any entrepreneur starting out.

To get started, you need someone to provide advice. How should you think about your customer? Should you license your technology? What sort of people do you need to hire? Where should you look to find funding? All these questions are difficult, and finding one experienced person who has done it all before, let alone a diversity of views that can allow you to hone the right answers, is unlikely to occur near the place you came up with your scientific breakthroughs. This is why so many people still "go west" in the United States—to Silicon Valley.[42] But even there, it is challenging to become embedded in a network.

Creating such a market is the mission of the Creative Destruction Lab (founded in Toronto by strategy professor Ajay Agrawal) that Joshua has been involved in. To create a market for judgment, you need to bring successful entrepreneurs together with science-based potential entrepreneurs. If it was just another networking event, this could be a one-day meet and greet. But to really create a market, you need deeper interaction. We found that even a three-month boot camp—the approach used by Y Combinator—wasn't sufficient. Instead, you need regular interaction over a year or more. That means getting people together in the right place, at the right time, so they are matched appropriately and then providing the seed for a long-term relationship. It is like a marriage market, but more akin to the way a religious institution matches couples than speed dating.

The returns for creating such markets are potentially high. Already we know that family relationships—one way entrepreneurs can acquire judgment in the absence of a market—can drive invention.[43] We also know that when innovative businesses bring more talent to a location, it can spur entrepreneurship, especially when there is a significant scientific research institution in the region.[44] This suggests that market creation can unlock scientific research that otherwise would sit dormant.

So how do you create a market where there isn't one? You move the missing bit to a single point in space—specifically, a lecture room at the University of Toronto's Rotman School of Management. Sitting at narrow

desks in U-shaped tiered seating are business mentors who have made suc-
cessful exits. In a recent cohort, they included Tony Lacavera, who sold his
Canadian cell phone network, Wind, for $1.3 billion. Next to him sat Michael
Hyatt, who sold his Canadian start-up for almost half a billion. Across the
room was William Tundstall-Pedoe. You may not have heard of him, but
you may have been heard of his invention, Alexa, which was acquired by
Amazon. At the next desk sat Anousheh Ansari, an entrepreneur of Ansari
XPRIZE fame. She has been to the International Space Station. Alongside her
was Barney Pell. His company, Moon Express, is going farther still.

The aim of the Rotman School's Creative Destruction Lab is to help
science-based entrepreneurs build their start-ups. This isn't an incubator. On
five occasions over the academic year, the group gathers for a day or two,
and then goes back to their jobs. The value for the entrepreneurs is that they
get an intense dose of guidance and advice from a group of successful mentors. In other words, they obtain the critical judgment they otherwise lack.

The room is a solution to a problem that has plagued entrepreneurial
programs everywhere but Silicon Valley. Entrepreneurs—especially science-
based ones—need advice. They have limited resources and not enough
time. Neither of these can be wasted. They come to find out what they
should focus on. Successful mentors have their opinions. Sometimes they
will disagree with one another. But the room has rules. Entrepreneurs need
to walk out with three objectives for the next two months and support from
at least one of these busy people over that time. Otherwise they won't be
back. The entrepreneurs get advice from a diverse and experienced set of
mentors, while the mentors are forced to come to an accord with each other
on their recommendations.

There are also some spectators in the room. Venture capitalists and angel
investors come in from around the world. Entrepreneurs are not always
seeking funding, but when they are, there is a liquid market right there.
Often millions of dollars of funding can be committed in minutes. Having
a capital market wasn't the initial objective of the program. But when you
have people spending time with ventures over the course of an academic
year, they get a picture of what they are dealing with. They don't just get
a snapshot but also a trajectory. They see the decisions, missed objectives,
and pivots. At each step, the risks are taken out of investments, just a little.

That has worked. When it started in 2013, the Creative Destruction Lab
had a goal of $50 million in equity creation in five years. With just fifteen

ventures getting through the program, that aim was considered audacious. In 2017, the collective value of the start-ups passed $2 billion. Yes, there were stars such as Waterloo's Thalmic Labs (now called North), whose wearable technologies are used by amputees, surgeons, and musicians. But there is also a long tail of success: more than 80 percent of the ventures that make it through the program are still going.

The Creative Destruction Lab has graduated four hundred ventures. Most of them came alive throughout their year. Validere, whose technology could assess the quality of liquids, entered the Creative Destruction Lab talking to cosmetics companies, and by its graduation was dealing with oil and hazardous waste. Nymi, with patents allowing for heartbeat authentication, quit its years-long efforts to license its technology and built its own wearable device.

Bridgit is upending project management on large building sites with an all-woman founding team. Fundmetric, in the difficult charitable fundraising space, uses artificial intelligence to improve donor targeting.[45] The Creative Destruction Lab shows it is possible to create missing markets for judgment. When it works, the result really is as exciting as finding a lost Rembrandt in your attic. The Creative Destruction Lab has since spread from its original home at the University of Toronto to new sites at the University of British Columbia, the University of Calgary, Dalhousie University, Université de Montréal, and Oxford University. There is a need for this type of organization in universities across the world.

Ten Ideas for Boosting Innovation

As we have noted, it is a myth to imagine that all innovation flows from the private sector. Governments have been responsible for many of the technological breakthroughs that we use every day. Through intellectual property laws, education programs, public sector research agencies, and research grants, governments can help make society more innovative.

But just because the public sector has successfully encouraged innovation, it hardly follows that every government innovation program will have a positive effect. A badly designed public sector program can be a waste of money—or worse, can discourage innovation. So we need to apply the same careful and creative spirit to public sector innovation programs that we apply to invention itself.

In our experience, too many proposals for increasing innovation start from the implicit presumption that smart people can predict the future. We're not that bold. In fact, we believe that any sensible suggestions to expand innovation must recognize the role that uncertainty plays in the world. If we knew for sure that "technology X" was going to be the next big thing, then it's likely that private investors would already have backed every promising start-up in the field. A wiser role for government is to acknowledge that some innovators will fail and to foster ongoing inquiry by as many great minds as possible. Not only is this the most efficient approach; it is also the most equitable one.

To this end, we propose ten ideas for boosting innovation.

1. *Encourage healthy competition between research funders.* Just as private sector competition fosters innovation, competition between grant-making agencies can create an incentive to add value to the most promising new research ideas. Critically, these agencies should be encouraged not to identify researchers already on the path to success, but rather to bend the research trajectory upward. Comparing those who just got grants with those who just missed out, the National Institutes of Health and the New Zealand Marsden Fund both appear to increase scientific output.[46] Another study finds that National Science Foundation grants boost output, but only for younger researchers.[47]

2. *Grants should foster moonshot innovation.* If research funders want big breakthroughs, then they need to take risks. In one study, a team of economists assessed grants provided by the Howard Hughes Medical Institute, which "urges its researchers to take risks, to explore unproven avenues, [and] to embrace the unknown—even if it means uncertainty or the chance of failure." The economists found that Howard Hughes Medical Institute grants led to more high-impact research than money provided by the National Institutes of Health, which operated on a more conventional model.[48] But it also turned out that the Hughes Institute sponsored more research that received zero citations. When research funders take risks, they can expect more rockets *and* more fizzers.

3. *Bring intellectual property laws into balance.* Intellectual property protection doesn't just encourage innovators; it can stymie them. Walt Disney's works are protected by copyright until 2036, seventy years after his death. It is difficult to see what new ideas were induced by the 1998

decision to increase copyright terms from life plus fifty years to life plus seventy years. There would be no net economic benefit to increasing copyright terms still further. In the area of patents, Alex Tabarrok proposes a hump-shaped innovation strength curve, in which patents initially increase innovation, and then as they get too strong, they begin to reduce innovation. From 1997 to 2017, Amazon's patent over one-click ordering gave it a monopoly on that basic idea. Tabarrok argues that we are on the wrong side of the innovation curve, and proposes variable duration patents—say, three, eight, or twenty years—in which the level of scrutiny by the patent examiner is stronger the longer the term requested.[49]

4. *Build innovation training for everyone.* While many countries' innovation strategies mention the importance of including women, people with disabilities, and those with low incomes, the reality is less promising.[50] Youngsters growing up in the leafy suburbs are more likely to learn science in school, have family friends who are innovators, attend college, and have easy access to an incubator environment. Government programs to encourage young entrepreneurs should explicitly target "lost Curies" by establishing themselves in disadvantaged neighborhoods. Our starting point as a society should be that clever ideas are just as likely to come from children born in Biloxi and Sioux Falls as those born in Boston and Silicon Valley.

5. *Use promises and prizes to encourage innovation.* In 2007, Canada, Italy, Norway, Russia, the United Kingdom, and the Bill and Melinda Gates Foundation committed US$1.5 billion to companies that could provide a vaccine to prevent pneumococcal disease. Known as an "advance market commitment," the group guaranteed pharmaceutical companies that it would buy millions of doses, so long as firms promised to keep the price at $3.50 per dose. Gavi, the Vaccine Alliance expects the decision to save the lives of up to 1.5 million children by 2020.[51] Other advance market commitments have been considered for Malaria and HIV.[52] Such incentives encourage diverse approaches to solve the world's thorniest problems and reduce the risk associated with embarking on such ventures.

6. *Beware of tax breaks.* From a political economy perspective, it can be tempting to reward innovation by reducing a firm's tax liability rather than by providing a grant. When a company gets a $100 tax deduction,

it doesn't show up on the government bottom line. But when a firm gets a $100 grant, it does appear as a government expense. Yet from a taxpayer's perspective, the two policies are of equal cost—and the advantage of the grant is that it is likely to be subject to greater public scrutiny. All advanced countries support business research and development, but some (such as Israel) focus on direct grants, while others (such as the Netherlands) concentrate on tax breaks.[53] While research and development tax incentives can help firms bring ideas to market, grants are a better way of encouraging high-risk, long-term breakthroughs.[54]

7. *Reduce barriers to entry for entrepreneurs.* Sometimes, markets are concentrated because the leading firms are better than the rest. But at other times, high market shares reflect high entry barriers. Competition policy that lowers entry barriers and switching costs is the best way of ensuring a level playing field for new entrants. For instance, we could achieve this in many digital networks by encouraging data and identity portability. Regulators should also be discouraged from taking an excessively conservative approach that stymies start-ups and encouraged to look at options like a regulatory sandboxes, which allow for small-scale experimentation. Because innovation is inherently uncertain, society can benefit massively by making it easier for those who want to try something new. Encouraging new entrants not only provides consumers more choice but also puts competitive pressure on existing firms to lift their game.

8. *Build catalytic networks and entrepreneurial ecosystems.* Innovation does not happen in a vacuum, and often the barriers to taking leading-edge science and translating it into useful technology are experience and judgment. Rather than picking winners, governments and private institutions need to encourage the matching of judgment with science to unlock potential entrepreneurs as well as innovative ideas. The Creative Destruction Lab shows that you can overcome the tyranny of geographic location by putting the entire ecosystem in a room at regularly scheduled intervals.

9. *Free up public sector and university science for innovation.* Much knowledge is produced within the public sector including by universities. Studies have shown that when researchers are free to pursue commercial opportunities for such research, more innovations result. In the United States, policies that assign rights to researchers remove frictions and create positive incentives to research in directions that favor commercial application.

10. *Update the national statistics.* Designing a statistical architecture that is fit for purpose sounds like a job for the wonkiest of wonks. But it matters. When news outlets splash big with a story about growth, inflation, or unemployment, they're relying on the experts to get the details right. Alas, as we mentioned in chapter 2, our statistical services were designed for an economy dominated by corn and steel, not cloud computing and smartphones. Job statistics can be distorted by the sharing economy. Price statistics struggle to incorporate massive changes in quality. Intangible investment is poorly captured.[55] In an era of instant feedback, it ought to be possible to move from backward-looking statistics to measures that let us know how the economy is performing today.

From forceps to intermittent wipers, Squatty Potties to dog watches (OK, maybe not the last one), inventors have improved our lives. In his book *Fifty Things That Made the Modern Economy*, economist Tim Harford documents how our world has been transformed by things that we so often take for granted, from the shipping container to air-conditioning, antibiotics to the bar code.[56] As he notes, these inventions had surprising and far-reaching consequences. Who knew the fridge would shape global politics or that barbed wire would open up new tracts of land to farming? We can't anticipate these specific changes, but we can do a better job of creating institutions that respond to technological breakthroughs. It is to this challenge that we now turn.

7 Providing Insurance

The 1967 film *The Graduate* sees Benjamin Braddock, the twenty-one-year-old protagonist of the movie, cornered at a cocktail party by Mr. McGuire, a friend of his parents. McGuire says to Braddock, "I just want to say one word to you. Just one word. ... Plastics." Needless to say, the hero ignores this life advice, opting instead to elope with the girl of his dreams.

The world today seems full of McGuires, keen to impress on the young Braddocks that they can predict the next new thing. Some say that it's vital to specialize in mathematics. Or health care. Or environmental technology. Or the blockchain.

We offer a different forecast. We predict that most of those who make confident bets about tomorrow's labor market will end up with egg on their faces. There's no modern-day equivalent of "plastics."

One way to see this is to recognize how uncertain the world's leading entrepreneurs are about the direction that their technologies will take. Musk has championed the "hyperloop," which would join cities like Los Angeles and San Francisco, carrying pods of passengers down vacuum tubes at six hundred miles per hour. If it works, the hyperloop could change the future of intercity transit—but no one knows right now if that will happen.

Similarly, Amazon's Jeff Bezos appears to still be in the process of considering how the company might approach brick-and-mortar stores.[1] It has had limited success with its Amazon Fresh model. Analysts are uncertain how Amazon will use the Whole Foods stores it acquired in 2017. Amazon's impact on retail could change the future of work for millions of cashiers, but it still isn't clear what the online retailer will do. As Bezos once put it in an interview, "Did I anticipate [what Amazon is] today and the current version of it? No."[2]

Today's generation isn't the first to face uncertainty about the future. In the 1700s, the United States was urbanizing, industrializing, and gaining its independence. And one of the men who was most influential in shaping the nation was also the one who was most relentlessly focused on learning new things: Benjamin Franklin.

The list of Franklin's successes is so long it is almost comical. He was an inventor as well as politician, diplomat, and author. He founded the University of Pennsylvania and Philadelphia's fire department, invented the lightning rod and bifocals, and helped draft the Declaration of Independence. But his successes were never guaranteed. Franklin grew up with sixteen siblings in a poor family.

What interests us about Franklin is his curiosity and the value he placed on acquiring new skills. With just two years of formal education, he relied on a careful practice of bettering himself by concentrating each week on one of thirteen "virtues." In an era when books were expensive, he set up a subscription library. He established a discussion group to explore interesting ideas. Franklin even taught himself to swim, at a time when few knew how.

Three centuries on, the challenge is to ensure that everyone has the opportunity to follow a similar path. By developing a broad portfolio of talents, Franklin had a form of "insurance" against the social changes that took place during his lifetime. In this sense, education can act as a buffer against social, economic, or global shocks.

Teaching: The Profession That Creates All Others

Over the past century, the *quantity* of education acquired by the typical person in the United States has almost doubled, from seven to thirteen years.[3] Primary schooling has become ubiquitous, finishing high school has become the norm, and half of all high school graduates start a four-year college degree (although less than two-thirds who commence manage to graduate within six years).[4]

But the increase in the *quality* of education has been less dramatic. Since the early 1970s, National Assessment of Educational Progress results suggest that US fourth graders have made solid gains in reading and mathematics (on a five-hundred-point scale, their test scores have risen by thirteen and twenty-five points, respectively).[5] The gains are smaller among eighth graders, whose scores have gone up by eight points in reading and nineteen points in math. And they are smaller still among twelfth graders, whose scores have risen by a statistically insignificant two points on both tests.

Part of the challenge in comparing test score results over time is that the composition of the class may change. This is true in a demographic sense (more students today speak a language other than English at home, and more children have college-educated parents) and in terms of who stays on to complete school (higher year twelve retention rates may bring down the average score).[6] Still, if educational quality had risen across the board, we would expect to see the biggest gains in the highest grades. Instead, the data show the opposite. The fact that the gains are largest among lower grades does suggest that part of the gains may be due to children being better prepared for school rather than representing true value added.

Other tests paint a similar picture. The Trends in International Mathematics and Science Study shows that US fourth- and eighth-grade students improved their mathematics performance over the two decades from 1995 to 2015.[7] But over a shorter period (from the mid-2000s to 2015), the OECD's Programme for International Student Assessment exam reported no significant change in the performance of US fifteen-year-olds.[8]

A major challenge for US education is the decline in teacher aptitude. Although commentators generally agree that "teacher quality" is the single most important determinant of what children learn in school, there has been a marked drop in the reading and math performance of those people who enter the teaching profession.[9] The typical new teacher in the United States is someone who was in the bottom half of the aptitude distribution in their own class.[10] Yes, there are still high-scoring teachers in the schooling system, but fewer than in the past. Yes, passion, grit, and empathy are also valuable teacher traits, but aptitude matters. Great teachers are more commonly those who aced a subject than those who barely passed.

To understand the fall in teacher quality, it is necessary to understand the labor market in the 1950s. Back then, rampant gender pay discrimination in law, medicine, business, and other professions meant that teaching was one of the few professions (along with nursing) open to female university graduates. Teaching wasn't free of discrimination, but it provided considerably better opportunities for talented women than other occupations. Consequently, the caliber of lawyers was lower, while the caliber of teachers was higher.

The reduction in gender pay discrimination was one of the great post-war advances in developed societies, boosting both equity and efficiency. Not only did it expand the opportunities available to women, but it raised output, because nondiscriminatory firms are more productive. Discrimination has not been eliminated, but because US businesses make better use of the talents of women, they are more dynamic now than in the *Mad Men* era. Yet the occupation that has suffered the most is teaching, which is no longer the career of choice for the most talented women graduating from college.

In considering how to raise teacher effectiveness, developed countries could do worse than to look to the performance of Finland, which routinely ranks near the top of the international test score league tables.

Admittedly, we should be skeptical of those whose education reform ideas seemed to boil down to "be like Finland." The problem is that it isn't clear which bit of Finland's approach we should replicate. Late school starting ages? Less homework? Long recess breaks? No school uniforms? Low levels of inequality? A logical language, in which words are pronounced as they are written? As Monty Python put it, "Finland, Finland, Finland—Finland has it all."[11]

But what's far more interesting than "Finland is great" is the fact that this is only really the story of the past generation. In the 1960s and 1970s, Finland was a middling performer on international tests.[12] It was only in the late 1970s that Finland embarked on a major push to raise the aptitude of new teachers.

One mark of the success of Finland's teaching push is that teacher education students are generally drawn from the top fifth of high school graduates. For every position in a teacher education course, there are around ten applicants. They are selected not only on academic excellence but also through an interview. Finnish teachers are highly regarded, with polls placing teaching as the nation's most admired profession.

Raising teacher effectiveness involved a suite of changes in Finland. Smaller teacher education providers were closed down. The remaining universities were forced to be more selective and rigorous. The government worked closely with the teacher union in implementing the changes. Teacher pay is about average for the OECD, and the wage gains to experience are relatively small.[13] Finland has no national system of teacher merit pay, though municipalities sometimes pay bonuses to high-performing teachers.

Finland also mandated master's degrees for all teachers, meaning that those who wanted to teach needed to study for a minimum of five years. Economists have generally been skeptical of the value of master's degrees, noting that long study periods can act as barriers, effectively discouraging talented people from entering a profession. Although some US states require new teachers to begin working toward their master's degree, there is little evidence that teachers with a master's degree do better in the classroom.[14]

Why was Finland's push for master's-trained teachers a success? One possibility is that Finnish master's degrees were more focused on improving teaching than those in other countries. For example, Finnish students studying to be a secondary school teacher spend one-third of their time during a master's degree teaching in schools. Another possibility is that Finland succeeded *despite* its emphasis on master's degrees. Once you select teacher education students from among your best high school graduates, it is plausible that what you do with them in the university is of secondary importance.

Indeed, this goes to a broader point. Once you select superstar teachers, many of the critical problems in education become less significant. Issues such as the curriculum, test score reporting, and the caliber of school leadership become less crucial the more effective our teachers are.

Economists estimate that the difference between good and bad teachers translates into $250,000-higher lifetime earnings for every child.[15] Summed across a class of 20 or more pupils, this means that terrific teachers are literally worth their weight in gold. But the best teachers don't just convey facts; they inspire a love of learning. Getting teacher quality right will pay off with higher returns to education—because a great education makes people more effective at their jobs, and because terrific schooling prepares people to learn new skills as the need arises. Quality education encourages young people to find a productive path—with one study reporting that a better school can halve the crime rate among high-risk youths.[16] From a human capital standpoint, a great teacher provides insurance against a changing labor market.

Vocational Training

"I might be an employer in Bavaria, but if I hire someone who was trained in Hamburg, I have confidence about what they know."[17]

In Berlin, Andrew is sitting at the offices of the German Confederation of Skilled Crafts. He is among the many international visitors interested in learning about the German vocational model. In an era when many developed nations are struggling with high youth unemployment and high dropout rates from apprenticeship programs, policy makers from around the world are looking to see what they can learn from Germany.

Across the vocational training system, Germany has over three hundred designated professions. If you want to become a baker, tailor, or renewable energy installer, then you need to undertake training that is specific to the particular trade—or craft. The qualifications are tightly regulated, and the training takes place both on the job and in formal institutions. To graduate, students must pass a national exam, involving both written questions and a practical examination. For qualified craftspeople, the confederation runs annual skill competitions—pitting the best glassblowers, leather smiths, or graphic designers against one another. The oversight bodies are tripartite, made up of employer, union, and government representatives.

The aim of the German system isn't just to produce well-trained crafts-people but to engender a sense of pride in their work too. A recent advertising campaign encourages young people to undertake trade training in a craft—known as *Handwerk*—using the tagline "Handwerk can get you everywhere." As one of our colleagues describes the difference when he moved from Germany to Britain, "In Germany, when a male carpenter meets a woman at the bar, he tells her he's a carpenter. In Britain, he tells her he's a Manchester United supporter."

Yet the German system is not without its limitations. As economist Ludger Woessmann points out, there is a trade-off between giving workers job-specific skills such as how to produce a certain product; and general skills such as communication, problem solving, and teamwork. While job-specific skills are only useful within a particular narrow occupation, general skills can be broadly handy across multiple occupations.

In the early part of a person's career, the German model has been especially good at ensuring a smooth transition from school to work and keeping down the youth unemployment rate. A young person who has only general skills might be a "jack-of-all-trades, master of none." But a young person who has undertaken training in one of Germany's many specific crafts will have a rigorous knowledge of that occupation.

If the labor market stayed static, then it would be game, set, and match to job-specific training. But the problem comes when technology and globalization cause professions to shrink, forcing people to retrain. At this point, narrowly specialized workers may struggle to acquire new qualifications. Woessmann's analysis of three "apprenticeship countries"—Austria, Germany, and Denmark—compares people with general education against those with vocational education. Until age fifty, employment rates are higher among vocationally educated workers, but after that age, those with general education are more likely to have a job—perhaps because educational breadth lets them shift into less physically demanding roles.[18] A similar pattern can be seen with earnings. As Woessmann observes, "Vocational education seems to facilitate the school-to-work transition, but at the same time reduce the adaptability of older workers to changing environments."[19] (As it happens, there is a similar pattern among US science majors: the wage returns to studying applied science at college decline over the lifecycle, while the earnings benefit of studying pure science rises through a person's career.[20])

Seen like this, it is less clear that there is a "good" or "bad" way of providing vocational education. The more the world is likely to change, the riskier it is to put your eggs in the basket of a single occupation. The value of the German apprenticeship system lies in its rigor, but a slightly different approach might provide young people with more flexibility. Woessmann points to the example of commercial apprenticeships, where Germany has more than thirty specific pathways, including separate programs for courier apprentices and logistics apprentices. By contrast, Switzerland has a single commercial apprenticeship program, which provides a common training core in the first two years, followed by a third and final year of specialized training. While the German apprenticeship system is better known internationally, the Swiss approach strikes us as better suited to an environment in which the world of work could suddenly shift. In the twenty-first century, vocational training must provide not only practical skills to perform today's jobs but also the foundational abilities to continue learning as the labor market evolves. A great vocational education gives today's craftspeople an insurance policy for tomorrow.

The Costs and Benefits of College

Since the end of World War II, the number of universities in the world has grown from five hundred to over ten thousand.[21] College has shifted from an elite to a mass participation activity. Tuition costs have risen. Many have begun to ask: is higher education worthwhile?

From a pure economic standpoint, the answer appears to be yes. In recent years, workers with a bachelor's degree earned 75 percent more than those with just a high school diploma. Over the course of a career, the wage premium of attending college exceeds $1 million.[22]

What about students who just scraped in? According to a recent study using data from Florida, college is worthwhile for them too.[23] Those on the margin of admission saw an earnings jump of 22 percent, well in excess of the cost of attending a university.

Yet the cost of college has loomed large for many students. In 2018–2019, tuition at Columbia University had a sticker price of $56,608 annually.[24] Similarly, the sticker price is $55,320 at the University of Southern California per year and $54,120 a year at Northwestern University. Adjusted for inflation, the average tuition at four-year colleges has more than doubled in the past thirty years.[25] Sixty-nine percent of families choosing a university eliminated at least one college due to cost—an 11 percentage point rise over the past decade.[26] Among students who dropped out of college, two in five cite financial pressures as the main reason.[27]

Tuition costs are certainly rising faster than inflation, but there are two facts that we have to bear in mind when discussing the price of a university. One is that most students don't pay the sticker price. For example, students pay nothing to attend Columbia University if their parents earn less than $60,000 and own typical assets. Net of financial aid and tax breaks, tuition is less than half the average sticker price.[28] In 2018–2019, the average *net* tuition and fees paid by full-time students at four-year institutions was $3,740 at public colleges and $14,610 at private nonprofit colleges.[29]

The other factor worth bearing in mind is that the biggest cost of a university isn't what students have to pay; it's what they have to forgo. By attending college, students are missing out on a regular wage. To get a sense of how much forgone earnings matter, we want to compare lost earnings to out-of-pocket tuition costs, which account for scholarships. In this comparison, we can ignore the cost of college room and board, since workers have their own living expenses. Recall that for a public four-year college, which is where most students go, net tuition and fees averaged $3,740. Even if they were working at the minimum wage, the forgone earnings would be almost four times as large as the out-of-pocket tuition costs. The average net tuition is costlier at private nonprofit institutions ($14,610), but that is still less than the earnings that most students would likely forgo.[30]

Add up the benefits, subtract the costs, and the rate of return on a bachelor's degree is a solid 15 percent, up from 10 percent in the 1970s. Average returns vary by college major, with engineering degrees delivering a 21 percent return, architecture a 14 percent return, and hospitality an 11 percent return.[31] But compared with investing in the stock, bond, or property markets, college still looks like a terrific deal. In dollar terms, associate's degrees produce a smaller wage return, but because their cost—in tuition and forgone earnings—is also significantly smaller, the average rate of return on a two-year associate's degree is also around 15 percent. (Naturally, these calculations exclude room and board, since those who choose not to attend college still need to pay living expenses.)

So what can we do to ensure that the cost of tuition does not deter capable students from enrolling? One promising initiative is to simplify the process of applying for financial aid. In an experiment with H&R Block, low-income parents whose children likely qualified for financial aid were invited to spend another ten minutes working with the tax professional to fill out most of the information required for the college financial aid form. The children of those who were selected were 8 percentage points more likely to attend college.[32] In recent years, some changes have been made to simplify the financial aid application process, but it remains daunting. As one financial aid administrator noted, "Low-income students are often first-generation college students and are intimidated by the verification process. They know very little, if anything about taxes or the IRS. Navigating the process is daunting because they don't always have the support of a parent to see it through."[33]

In their book *The Student Loan Mess*, Joel and Eric Best estimate that US graduates owe $1 trillion in university loans, and that this amount is growing at a rate of $100 billion a year. They calculate that the current default rates are 15 to 20 percent, and project that the default rate will double in the future.[34] It is hard to see such a system as anything other than a failure.

Other countries take a different approach to college tuition. Since 1989, Australian college students have paid through an income-contingent loan. Debts are repaid through the tax system, and repayments only commence when students begin earning more than the average wage. If a college graduate never earns more than average, they never repay. If they lose their job, the repayments stop. If they move overseas, they are expected to report their worldwide income and make repayments if they are above the earnings threshold. The debt is indexed to keep pace with inflation, but there is no additional interest charge. In Australia, repayments are from 4 to 8 percent of a graduate's earnings, and the debt amounts to around half the cost of providing the education. Since almost all universities are public, the other half of the costs is largely covered by general taxation revenue.

The intellectual origins of income-contingent loans go back to Friedman in the 1950s, but it took Australian economist Bruce Chapman to persuade his government that they could be practically implemented in his country. Income-contingent loans for higher education now exist in several other countries, including New Zealand, South Africa, Hungary, South Korea, England, and Wales. A bill to institute them in the United States was proposed in Congress in 2013, but has since lapsed.[35]

Lifelong Learning

In 2008, University of Manitoba computer science professors Stephen Downes and George Siemens launched an open-access, online course called Connectivism and Connective Knowledge. With twenty-two hundred sign-ups, it was the world's first massive open online courses (MOOC). In 2012, the "year of the MOOC," three major initiatives were launched: Coursera (Stanford), edX (Harvard and MIT), and Udacity (independently run). Since then, take up has steadily grown, with around seventy million people a year now registering for a MOOC.

In 2014, Georgia Tech, whose computer science program regularly ranks in the nation's top ten, began offering its master's in computer science online, at a cost of $7,000—a fraction of the $45,000 paid by in-person students.[36] According to a careful study of the online program, most students wouldn't otherwise enroll in person. Georgia Tech's online students outperform in-person students on exams and have similar completion rates. Today, Georgia Tech online students account for around 7 percent of all master's in computer science graduates in the nation. A seven-week artificial intelligence course offered by fast.ai has now trained over a hundred thousand people to program deep learning models. One graduate, Sara Hooker, had no prior experience in deep learning, and on graduation, managed to get a place in Google's artificial intelligence residency program.[37]

From an insurance perspective, MOOCs provide a flexible option for people to pick up new skills as the economy changes. We think of lifelong learning as the ability to keep upgrading the software in our brain as we go through life. The old model of education—in which workers received a single dose of education at the start of their careers—was a bit like the handheld *Donkey Kong* games of the 1980s. *Donkey Kong* came in a sealed plastic case, and the software couldn't be upgraded. The new model—in which workers acquire new skills as they need them—is more like the way your smartphone automatically downloads new updates.

The popularity of the MOOC model of online learning cuts across a wide range of subjects. Class Central, a discovery platform for online courses, reports that its twenty-five most common searches in 2017 were "python, machine learning, java, data science, human resources, english, writing, deep learning, psychology, c, marketing, statistics, excel, javascript, spanish, law, french, photography, music, sql, digital marketing, finance, project management, design, [and] data."[38] Udacity's "nanodegrees" include Artificial Intelligence, partnering with IBM Watson; Self Driving Car Engineer, partnering with Mercedes-Benz; Data Analyst, partnering with Kaggle; and VR Developer, partnering with Google VR. The platforms that deliver MOOCs can be nimbler in response to market demands than traditional universities and vocational training institutions.

One of the challenges of traditional lifelong learning has been that it costs too much—in money and time. MOOCs tackle both problems. Course prices range from nothing to a few hundred dollars a month, with automated grading and peer assessment taking the place of traditional feedback systems. Courses are becoming shorter and more flexible; what would once have been a twelve-week online course with hard deadlines is now more likely to be offered as three four-week courses with flexible deadlines.[39] One commentator likens the shift to the unbundling of music through iTunes and Spotify, which has seen customers shift from buying albums to purchasing individual songs.[40] Many learners simply seek out an explainer video. Every day, half a billion people watch a how-to video on YouTube, where they learn everything from how to debone a fish to how to jack up a Ford F-150.[41]

A few years ago, Udacity cofounder Sebastian Thrun predicted that in fifty years' time, there will only be ten higher education institutions in the world—one of which could be Udacity.[42] We doubt that MOOCs will replace universities, but we do think that they will be fundamental to on-the-job training. Right now, MOOCs still face problems: high dropout rates, scrappy discussion forums, assessment processes that are vulnerable to fraud, worse outcomes for disadvantaged students, and a hodgepodge of credentials that lack the ready recognition of university qualifications.[43] But for all this, MOOCs are likely to be a major part of the way that tomorrow's workers retrain for jobs that do not exist today.

Free to Change

In 2006, Michael Devine worked as a computer scientist for the tech giant Adobe.[44] As a programmer in his late thirties, Devine was always on the lookout for new and exciting job opportunities. But strangely, for a reputable computer scientist at a major firm, the offers weren't flooding in.

Four years later, Michael found out why. It turned out that his company had entered into a secret agreement with a handful of other tech giants— Apple, Google, Intel, Intuit, and Pixar—not to hire each other's workers. In an angry phone call, Apple's Jobs had warned Google's Sergey Brin, "If you hire a single one of these people, that means war."[45]

Realizing this, Devine joined sixty-four thousand programmers filing a class action lawsuit, which ultimately led to a hefty settlement. Unfortunately it was only the tip of the iceberg. Soon after, the online retailers eBay and Intuit were caught doing the same thing. So were the film producers Lucasfilm and Pixar. It wasn't just the tech giants either. Hospitals had agreements to fix the pay and conditions for temporary nurses. Fashion designers were caught trying to reduce the pay and conditions for models.

In the job market, we can think of the ability to shift to a different employer or start your own firm as a kind of insurance policy. If you have a falling-out with your boss, it helps to have a good exit option. But it's not just illegal behavior by employers that makes this hard for workers. Many employees have a clause in their contracts that says if they leave, then for a specified period of time, they are forbidden from taking a job with a competing firm.

No one is suggesting that departing workers should be able to abscond with secret information, such as client lists or confidential design drawings. But noncompete clauses go further. In effect, they temporarily ban people from working in the industry where they have the most expertise. One in five US workers are currently bound by a noncompete agreement, and two in five have signed a noncompete agreement at some point in their careers.[46]

As well as making it harder for workers to switch to a better job, noncompete clauses stifle start-ups. Since many new companies are created by employees who leave to start a competing company, noncompete clauses reduce innovation. Using three decades of US patent data, economists found a "brain drain" of inventors from states that enforce noncompete clauses to states that do not.[47] Another study finds that noncompete clauses affect the entire work environment, with even workers who are not bound by such clauses suffering from reduced mobility, lower wages, and less job satisfaction.[48]

Alan Krueger, a prolific economist who died unexpectedly this year, did important work highlighting some of the most egregious examples of noncompete clauses. Amazon warehouse workers must agree that for eighteen months after working for the company, they will not join another firm that makes or sells something that "competes or is intended to compete with any product or service sold, offered or otherwise provided by Amazon." (Can you think of a product *not* sold on Amazon?) Sandwich store Jimmy John's used to ban its employees from working in other sandwich stores for up to three years after leaving Jimmy John's. Until 2018, franchise agreements for McDonald's contained "no poach" clauses, preventing managers from hiring staff who had worked at another McDonald's in the previous six months.[49] In each case, workers' careers suffer, as they end up with lower wages and less fulfilling work.

Noncompete clauses are just one way that firms can exert excessive power over employees. Two recent economic studies have calculated the degree to which hiring power was concentrated in a few firms.[50] Breaking the United States down into specific labor markets by occupation and geography—such as accountants in Kansas City—they find a considerable degree of concentration. When employees have fewer firms to choose from, wages are lower. The finding isn't a slam dunk, since another factor (such as the underlying productivity of the local labor force) might be correlated both with the number of firms in an area and the prevailing wage rate. But it does suggest that firms may often command labor markets just as they control product markets. This "monopsony power" (when a buyer dominates a market) hurts workers in the same way that monopoly power (when a seller dominates a market) can hurt customers.

When a few firms dominate the hiring process, they exert excessive power over the workforce. This means earnings stagnate, and can even cause some people to drop out of the labor market. Just as "one-company towns" have traditionally constrained opportunities for workers, monopsony power may exacerbate inequality. A lack of career opportunities also creates risks for employees, who can become so specialized in a single firm's way of doing business that they risk becoming unemployable if their company goes bust. Recent estimates suggest that monopsony power is likely exerting a huge drag on the economy.[51] One set of scholars likens the effect to a "wage-suppression" tax, but with the difference that the "tax" revenue is then thrown away. If monopsony hiring power was eliminated from the US labor market, they argue that median wages would rise by at least one-third. In 2018, economists puzzled at the fact that 4 percent unemployment did not lead to larger wage rises. Monopsony power is likely to be part of the answer.

Another barrier to job shifting is occupational licensing. When Essence Farmer moved from Maryland to Arizona, she assumed that she could continue her work braiding hair. But she discovered that Arizona required hair braiders to obtain a cosmetology license, which would have taken around sixteen hundred hours to acquire.[52]

Since the 1950s, the share of US workers covered by licensing laws has grown from one in twenty to one in four.[53] Tour guides, interior designers, tree trimmers, florists, travel agents, and furniture upholsterers are among more than one hundred professions that require a license in parts of the United States. These requirements are often inconsistent. For example, most states do not require locksmiths to have a license, but New Jersey law stipulates that locksmiths undertake two years of education and experience. In Connecticut, manicurists are not required to be licensed, while in Alabama, they must undertake 175 days of training.[54]

Occupational licensing can protect public safety. It's reassuring to know that pilots, doctors, and structural engineers have been accredited. But the safety argument is less clear for florists, decorators, and taxidermists. In one extreme example, the monks of Saint Joseph Abbey were prevented from selling wooden funeral caskets by Louisiana licensing laws.[55] They had to sue the state to overturn the funeral directors' monopoly on selling caskets. Moreover, if the public safety were really threatened by unlicensed occupations, then it is hard to see how wildly inconsistent state laws are protecting the public.

Analyzing the growth in occupational licensing, economists have found little evidence that it has improved quality, safety, or health, but significant evidence that it has increased prices.[56] According to one estimate, if an occupation is subject to licensing in a given state, labor supply drops by as much as one-quarter.[57] Occupational licensing also acts as a barrier to worker mobility.[58] Jason Furman, who served as President Obama's top economist, points out that licensing laws might be part of the reason that interstate mobility has been falling. Licensed workers are significantly less likely to move across state lines than workers in occupations that do not require a license. Licensing restrictions, Furman argues, "should be closely targeted to protecting public health and safety, and should not be overly broad or burdensome."[59]

The Independent Worker

TaskRabbit engages people to do some unusual things. Sam Ridley served as a microphone runner at a UN conference in New York City. Katie Zechar steam cleaned "Weird Al" Yankovic's outfits ahead of the entertainer's San Francisco show. A woman in Los Angeles didn't want to attend a birthday party of someone she barely knew, so she hired an amateur actor to go along and pretend to be her.[60]

Platforms such as TaskRabbit, GrubHub, Uber, and Lyft are part of the fast-growing "sharing" or "gig" economy. Although only about 1 percent of the workforce are gig economy workers, that proportion is growing as ride sharing replaces taxis, food delivery becomes centralized, and customers recognize that they can pay for small tasks.[61] Need your IKEA furniture assembled? Try Handy. Like a personalized tour while you're in a new city? Check out Vayable. Keen for a privately cooked meal in the home of a chef? Perhaps you should try Eatwith. Want a document translated? Gengo. These platforms establish a triangular relationship between themselves, their customers, and the people who do the work.

Yet while the growth of the gig economy is a boon for consumers, it poses challenges for workers. Even multiple sharing economy jobs may not allow workers to earn enough to buy a house or raise a family. Moreover, these jobs tend to be risky. Gig economy workers often lack health insurance and retirement savings. They may be vulnerable to discrimination, and unable to bargain for better pay and conditions.

Writing for the Brookings Institution's Hamilton Project, economists Seth Harris and Alan Krueger argue that part of the problem arises from applying new modes of work to old categories of employment.[62] Traditionally, workers have either been "employees" or "contractors." Employees give up autonomy at work in exchange for a package of protections, including minimum pay rates, discrimination protection, workplace safety, and Social Security contributions. Independent contractors decide when and where they work, buy their own equipment, and choose whether or not to contract for new work. With control comes risk; contractors hope to make a profit, but know that they could also end up in the red.

When it comes to employment and taxation laws, gig economy workers are typically classified as independent contractors, but sometimes the law deems them to be employees. Because the tests are not consistent across all aspects of employment law, there is even a risk that a worker in the gig economy may be "deemed entitled to the minimum wage, but not to have her employer pay half of her payroll taxes."[63] By assuming that the categories of employee and independent contractor cover the field, there is a risk that platforms may deliberately organize themselves in order to leave workers without protection. Judges are still figuring out precisely where to draw the line, with a 2018 California Supreme Court decision replacing the previous multifactor employment test with a simpler one: whether a job is part of the "usual course" of the firm's business. Based on this, drivers at delivery firm Dynamex were deemed to be employees rather than contractors.[64]

Right now, judges have to choose between two categories. But the real problem is that gig economy workers are neither traditional employees nor conventional independent contractors. A platform such as Fiverr might specify the task to be performed, the payment amount, and the time frame. It is left up to the employee to work out whether they want the job, and how to do it. Gig economy workers are rarely required to wear a uniform, but they are vulnerable to being dropped if the platform decides that their customer ratings have fallen below the expected threshold.

Harris and Krueger propose a new category: the independent worker. Independent workers would receive some of the benefits of employees, including health insurance, retirement accounts, payroll withholding, civil rights protections, an opt-in program for workers' compensation insurance, and the freedom to organize and collectively bargain.[65] But they would not be eligible for the full package of benefits that employees receive. The main focus of the category of independent workers would be those working in the gig economy, but it might also include more traditional occupations such as direct sales workers and taxi drivers who lease their vehicles.

The 51 Percent

Lilly Ledbetter was born in Possum Trot, Alabama, in a house without electricity or running water. In 1979, with two small children at home, she applied for a job as supervisor at a Goodyear Tire and Rubber plant. She got the job—one of the first women hired by Goodyear—and worked there for the next two decades.

Toward the end of her time at Goodyear, Ledbetter began to suspect that she was earning less than her male colleagues. An anonymous note in her mailbox confirmed it. Despite being praised by her bosses, she had been given smaller raises than the men who worked around her. Over the course of her time at Goodyear, pay discrimination cost Ledbetter more than $200,000. Her experience led President Obama to sign the Lilly Ledbetter Fair Pay Restoration Act, which covers the kind of systematic underpayment experienced by Ledbetter.

Pay discrimination is often regarded as a "women's issue," but it goes further than that. Injustice at work undermines the sense of fairness that is fundamental to a healthy workplace. Employees are less productive when they perceive their working environments to be unfair.[66] Institutional forces that limit the ability of women to work create a situation in which families have less flexibility to juggle work and child raising, or respond to economic change by acquiring new skills. A society that doesn't provide sufficient economic opportunities for 51 percent of the population will be more unequal and less responsive to technological change.

To see the challenge, it is helpful to compare the United States with other advanced countries. In the mid-1980s, women's employment rates in France and the United States were similar. Today, French women are nearly 10 percentage points more likely to be employed than US women.[67] And although the US gender pay gap has narrowed since the 1970s, women's hourly wages are still 16 percent lower than men's.[68] Hold constant age, race, education, and occupation, and the gap is 15 percent. In other words, the typical woman needs to work for seventy minutes to earn what the typical man earns in an hour.

A large portion of the gender pay gap is related to women taking career breaks or "downshifting" when they have children.[69] So a crucial factor in closing the gender pay gap is reducing "child penalties" by providing more affordable childcare. Economists have shown that increasing childcare subsidies has a strong impact on helping women combine paid work and motherhood. This holds whether the subsidies are provided to parents or centers. Better childcare offers a promising way to reverse the significant drop in employment rates among low-educated married mothers (such women were 13 percentage points less likely to work in 2016 than in 2000).[70]

Paid leave matters too. The United States is the only advanced nation not to offer universal paid parental leave.[71] Parents are also constrained by the fact that many cannot use their earned sick leave to support an ill family member. These issues can be readily fixed and would deliver significant economic dividends.

Other causes of the gender gap are more challenging to address. When single mother Jacquelyn Hines began work at New Breed Logistics, a supply chain logistics company in Memphis, she found herself reporting to a supervisor who had a habit of making sexually explicit comments to Hines and her female coworkers.[72] One day, he pressed his crotch into a woman's back. Women who complained about his behavior were fired.

Surveys find that one in four women have, like Hines, experienced sexual harassment in the workplace. Yet nine times out of ten, victims do not file a formal complaint, opting instead to avoid the harasser or leave the company. Despite the fact that harassment is ethically and legally wrong, the lack of support for those who report it means that harassment continues to impose a massive cost not just on victims but also on society as a whole. Among the strategies that seem to reduce harassment are clear leadership from management to create a safe workplace culture, reporting policies that ensure complaints are followed up and treated as confidential where possible, and training that encourages bystanders to speak out against the harassment of coworkers.[73]

Another systematic factor that exacerbates the gender participation gap is joint tax filing. Since 1948, married couples have been treated as a single tax unit, with their income pooled for tax purposes. The effect of this is that the lower-earning member of the couple (typically the woman) faces the same marginal tax rate as her higher-earning spouse.[74] In a progressive tax system, this acts as a deterrent for women entering the workforce. It would be worth considering whether the United States should follow the example of Britain and New Zealand, which changed their tax codes to fully individual filing in order to remove this disincentive. According to one estimate, such a switch would boost employment for married women by nine percent (and raise the marriage rate by eight percent).[75]

How does technology affect the gender pay gap? In her 2014 Presidential Address to the American Economic Association, Claudia Goldin pointed to the intriguing fact that occupations with a high part-time penalty also appeared to have a large gender pay gap.[76] In law, part-time attorneys earn lower hourly wages than full-time attorneys. Law is also a profession where the pay gap between women and men is large. Conversely, pharmacists have virtually no part-time penalty, with part-time pharmacists getting the same hourly wages as full-time pharmacists. Correspondingly, male and female pharmacists earn similar hourly wages.

Part of the explanation, Goldin argues, is "the extensive use of computer systems that track clients across pharmacies, insurance companies, and physicians mean that any licensed pharmacist knows a client's needs as well as any other. If a pharmacist is assisting a customer and takes a break, another can seamlessly step in. In consequence, there is little change in productivity for short-hour workers and for those with labor force breaks." Other occupations, including optometrists and veterinarians, are taking advantage of larger practices and better computer systems to reduce the prevalence of long and unpredictable hours.

Elsewhere, technology is having the opposite effect. In mid-2014, Starbucks worker Jannette Navarro found herself scheduled to work until 11 p.m. on Friday night, then start again at 4 a.m. on Saturday, and report on Sunday morning at 5 a.m. She would often find out her schedule just a few days beforehand, causing chaos as she looked for care for her four-year-old son and tried to attend community college classes. Meanwhile, an executive at the company that designed Starbucks' staff-scheduling software extolled the way that the technology helped cut labor costs: "It's like magic."[77]

While Starbucks now gives its employees more notice of when they will be working, other firms continue to automate their schedules, failing to ask workers their preferences and offering no compensation when a shift is canceled.[78] Nearly half of part-time workers say they get only a week's notice of their schedule.[79] This particularly harms women, who are more likely to be juggling work and family. Inflexible jobs are the antithesis of the insurable future that we favor.

The Balance between Work and Home

At the heart of gender equity is the work-home balance. The United States is the only major advanced economy without a mandated system of paid parental leave. Although some larger corporations and public entities offer paid leave, many employers do not. Consequently, US women, in particular, face especially difficult tradeoffs in combining paid work with child raising.

On the employer side, in spite of its other potential merits—in terms of health or child development—mandated paid parental leave would represent a cost. Because women are more likely to take such leave than men, the expectation of those costs can potentially lead to employment discrimination against women—even those who do not plan to have children.[80]

The challenge is how to provide help for parents without exacerbating inequalities in the labor market. One possibility for the United States would be to introduce a right to paid parental leave and provide employers with a strong incentive to reintegrate workers who took advantage of such leave. A "return-to-work" tax credit might give employers a 150 percent tax credit on the salary of a returning parent. This would put the onus on employers to provide a flexible workplace. But it would also reduce the cost to companies employing workers who take parental leave. Instead, firms would have an incentive to support returning workers. This is because a returning worker would be cheaper for them than hiring a new one. Policy makers need to grapple with the causes of labor market inequalities head-on when devising good social policies. A return-to-work tax credit is one option that we believe should be on the table in the United States.[81]

Making Work Pay

Sanjuana lives in Buncome County, North Carolina, with her husband and their three young children. Because her husband works in landscaping, the winter months can be tough, and the family sometimes gets behind in paying bills. Then, at tax time, the family claims a wage subsidy called the Earned Income Tax Credit (EITC). As Sanjuana puts it, "If we did not have that money we would be at risk of losing our trailer lot. We paid the minimum throughout the year, and then paid the remainder at tax time."[82]

Created in 1975, the EITC is one of the most effective antipoverty programs in the United States. For families earning below about $50,000 (the exact upper limit depends on marital status and the number of children in the household), it provides a tax refund that can be worth as much as $6,577 a year. For many families, including Sanjuana's, the credit helps push them above the poverty line. Because EITC recipients are less likely to be on welfare, and more likely to pay sales and payroll taxes, it ends up saving money on other government programs. Once this is considered, every dollar that the government spends on the EITC has a true cost of just 13¢.[83]

Historically, the EITC has enjoyed support from Democratic lawmakers (who like its focus on alleviating poverty and assisting children) and Republican legislators (who like the fact that it encourages work). Yet even though it is the most successful program for preventing child poverty, it could do more. One proposal involves boosting the EITC for one-child families (the largest recipient group) to put them on par with households that have two children.[84] Another suggestion is to increase the EITC for childless workers, who presently receive a maximum of $529.

We believe that boosting in-work benefits targeted to the poorest is a better approach than the frequently touted "universal basic income." Work provides not only income but a sense of purpose and dignity too. One way to see this is to analyze life satisfaction data, which lets us measure the impact on happiness of becoming unemployed. Looking across tens of thousands of people, it is possible to compare unemployed people with individuals who are similar on all other dimensions—including income. This suggests that in order to be just as happy as someone with a job, an unemployed person would need an income boost of $60,000.[85] In other words, a person would be equally happy if they had a job paying $40,000 as if they were unemployed with $100,000 in non-wage income.

The decrease in overall life satisfaction that comes with unemployment is enormous. Holding household income constant, the reduction in happiness from job loss is around two-thirds as large as the reduction in happiness that accompanies marital separation or widowhood. Across countries, those nations with low employment rates tend to have lower average levels of reported life satisfaction.[86] We should not give up on the notion of a society in which most prime-aged adults are gainfully employed.

Our other concern with a universal basic income is that each dollar of government transfers does less to reduce inequality than in a system of targeted payments. It's difficult to see why Oprah Winfrey and Michael Bloomberg need a government payment. By giving welfare to those who are not at risk of poverty, a universal basic income would increase the degree of "churn" in the tax and transfer system. While estimates of the cost of churn vary, it is plausible that the cost of raising $1 of revenue is around 30¢.[87] If it was simply taxed back from most recipients, a universal basic income would be universally costly to the economy.

Ten Ideas for Reducing Inequality

Sometimes, Okun's famous trade-off between equity and efficiency applies. There are moments when policy makers must choose between growth and fairness, between increasing overall output and sharing it more equally between people.

But as with our innovation-boosting proposals in the previous chapter, this trade-off does not apply to most of the ideas below. Improving the quality of education for disadvantaged children will make businesses more profitable, reduce crime, and curb inequality. Curtailing sexual harassment in the workplace is not only a matter of justice but also of productivity. And so on.

Here are ten ideas to reduce inequality.

1. *Make teacher effectiveness the top schooling priority*. For all the talk about teacher quality being the number one factor in school effectiveness, teacher effectiveness risks getting lost in the weeds of a host of other agendas. We believe that raising teacher effectiveness should be the core focus of schooling policy. Following the lead of Finland, the United States can shift over a generation to a point where teaching is considered an elite occupation, drawing new teachers largely from the top tenth of the class.

2. *Boost the quality of vocational training*. Several continental European countries have a strong tradition of rigorous apprenticeship programs, which are tested through national exit exams. Among these, Germany is the best known for the pride it engenders in its craftspeople. Yet having hundreds of separate trade streams, as Germany does, risks locking tradespeople into declining occupations. We believe that the Swiss approach of providing a smaller set of broadly based apprenticeships would be more appropriate to a changing labor market.

3. *Simplify college loans*. The current US college loan application system is too complex. The young people most likely to be deterred are those

from low-income and minority backgrounds, or where no one else in the family has attended college. Simplifying the current financial assistance process would be a useful first step, but a better long-term strategy would be to shift from the current government-backed loan system to an Australian-style income contingent loans scheme in which repayments are made through the tax system, and only in years when graduates earn above the average wage.

4. *Encourage MOOCs.* As IBM boss Ginni Rometty notes, "Some jobs will be displaced, but 100 percent of jobs will be augmented by artificial intelligence." That means switching "from education as a content transfer to learning as a continuous process."[88] We believe that governments can boost the uptake of MOOCs by recognizing appropriate online qualifications in their hiring process, encouraging graduate schools to take MOOC qualifications into account, and accrediting online institutions.[89] One possible model is the "Lisbon Recognition Convention," signed by over fifty countries and encouraging flexible pathways by allowing course credits to be transferred across universities.[90]

5. *Ban noncompete clauses.* Perhaps the best argument for banning noncompete clauses from US employment agreements is that one of the most innovative places on the planet—California—does not allow them. California law invalidates contract clauses that restrain anyone "from engaging in a lawful profession, trade, or business" (this ban helps explain why six technology giants instead entered into a secret agreement not to hire each other's workers).[91] Google, Apple, and Facebook are all headquartered in California, despite the fact that they cannot use noncompete clauses in their employment agreements. Indeed, the ban on noncompete clauses is one factor that spurred the growth of Silicon Valley.

6. *Limit occupational licensing.* Concerns about the growth of occupational licensing span the ideological spectrum, from Democrats like Jason Furman to libertarians such as the Institute for Justice. Occupational licenses should be targeted toward protecting public health and safety. New proposals for occupational licenses should be automatically reviewed after several years. Where an occupation does need to be licensed, states should set up mutual recognition schemes so that workers are not deterred from moving across state lines to find a better job.[92]

7. *Create a new employment category: independent workers.* In the shared or gig economy, the unusual relationship between customers, platforms, and providers means that the traditional dichotomy between employees and contractors is outdated. Governments should create a new category of independent US workers, who would then receive some of the benefits of employees, including the freedom to collectively bargain, health insurance, retirement accounts, payroll withholding, discrimination protections, and an opt-in program for workers' compensation insurance.

8. *Raise the EITC.* Unlike a universal basic income, the EITC rewards work, is targeted at the most vulnerable, and costs a whole lot less. The policy has been proven to raise test scores among recipient children and cut the poverty rate. Any increase in the EITC would be desirable, but we particularly favor increasing the credit for childless workers and those with just one child.

9. *Encourage technologies that make jobs more family friendly.* While there will always be some jobs that require workers to work long or unpredictable hours, the example of pharmacy has shown that the savvy use of technology can reduce the part-time penalty and thereby narrow the gender pay gap. But it is also important to guard against the risk that worker-scheduling algorithms will be used to make some jobs more family *unfriendly*. One way to achieve this would be to require that employees have a right to be consulted on shift changes and compensated for last-minute cancellations.[93]

10. *Reform benefits, taxes, and employment law to remove biases against working women.* The United States should join the rest of the advanced world in offering paid parental leave—ideally in a form that enables either parent, regardless of gender, to take time off. Work-friendly parental leave could take the form of a bonus payment when the primary carer returns to work—encouraging new parents to stay engaged with the labor force. US childcare subsidies should be boosted and the tax system reformed so as to reduce tax rates on secondary earners. In the workplace, bosses should be encouraged to create a culture in which sexual harassment is treated as a serious offense, including through training bystanders to step in when they spot inappropriate behavior.

In forming our policy recommendations for tackling inequality, we are acutely conscious that Knightian uncertainty applies to policy solutions just as it does to technological innovation. As a recent report from the Laura and John Arnold Foundation observed, policy makers have launched many well-intentioned initiatives to tackle social problems, but many have been "guessing at the solutions."[94] Unfortunately, when subjected to rigorous evaluations such as randomized trials, most new programs don't produce the hoped-for effects.[95] While we have done our utmost to identify programs that are backed by rigorous evaluations, we urge policy makers to consider rolling out programs in a way that allows them to be subject to a randomized evaluation. The best way to deal with fundamental policy uncertainty is to build a better feedback loop.

We began this chapter with the stories of two Benjamins—*The Graduate* character Benjamin Braddock, who ignored the advice to go into plastics, and founding father Benjamin Franklin, the original lifelong learner. While most parents would encourage their children to follow Franklin rather than Braddock, we think that both have something to teach us. In an uncertain world, we need systems that will encourage everyone to keep acquiring new skills. But we also need to build a world in which people can follow their heart and chase their dreams—safe in the knowledge that failure won't bring disaster.

.

Conclusion

In January 1943, the United States banned the sale of sliced bread. The nation was at war, and Food Administrator Claude Wickard explained to the public that preslicing bread not only encouraged people to eat more of it but also required that the loaf be more heavily wrapped.

The public were not impressed. Having to cut the bread took longer—particularly in a household that ate toast for breakfast and sandwiches for lunch. Seven weeks later, the government relented, and sliced bread returned.

The public reaction to the ban on sliced bread showed how quickly people had embraced this new innovation. It was only in 1928 that Otto Rohwedder invented the first bread-slicing machine, and it took two more years before Wonder Bread began to market the product nationwide. But the original bakeries in Missouri promoted sliced bread as "the greatest forward step in the baking industry since bread was wrapped." Millions of Americans agreed.

New inventions have unexpected consequences. Sliced bread saved time for households across the country. It also drove up bread consumption and made households significantly more sensitive to changes in the government-mandated price of bread. Once the new innovation had become part of people's lives, the government could not address its effects with a simplistic attempt to reverse the technological change. It had to think differently.

In this book, we take the same approach to innovation. Ours is not a stuff-the-genie-back-in-the-bottle approach but an attempt to think rigorously about how society should adapt to a world of rapid innovation. Our twin benchmarks for success are a reduction in the gap between rich and poor, and an increase in the number of valuable inventions.

Two long-dead economists are fundamental to how we think about the problem. The first is Schumpeter—Austrian finance minister, Harvard professor, and putative achiever in the fields of horsemanship and amorous affairs. Schumpeter characterized capitalism as "an evolutionary process of continuous innovation and 'creative destruction.'"[1]

In our experience, there are only two groups of people who aren't uncomfortable when they hear the phrase creative destruction: the selfish and the inattentive. Once you've pondered the problem for a bit, creative destruction *should* make you uneasy, because it reminds us that even the simplest creations can destroy the jobs of those around us.

Take wheeled suitcases. In 1970—more than four thousand years after the invention of the wheel—Bernard Sadow was picking up his luggage at Boston airport on his way back from a family holiday in Aruba. An executive at a Massachusetts company that made coats and luggage, Sadow saw a worker rolling a large machine on a wheeled skid. He told his wife: "That's what we need for luggage." The idea hit some early snags, with many retailers saying that men would not roll their luggage (as Sadow notes, "It was a very macho thing").[2] But within a decade or two, virtually every suitcase featured Sadow's wheels. The creation was terrific for the typical traveler, yet as Schumpeter might have predicted, it was terrible for those who worked as airport porters.

The second dead economist whose ideas underpin this book is Knight—who came up with the distinction between risk (not knowing what you'll pull out when you put your hand into a bag containing half crisp and half rotten apples) and uncertainty (not knowing what share of the apples in the bag are rotten). Unlike us, many other people who write about the future of work tend to behave like weather forecasters. If you ask them about the prospects of a specific occupation a decade from now, they'll tell you that there's a 70 percent chance it has a sunny future, and a 30 percent chance of storms.

If only it were that easy. When weather forecasters are predicting tomorrow's skies, they're analyzing a closed system. Feeding thousands of pieces of data into supercomputers, they look for patterns that have historically predicted a given kind of weather and use their models to estimate the probabilities that you'll need your umbrella tomorrow. Sure, there are complications—from rare events like tsunamis to the volatility-increasing effects of climate change. But in general, their models are pretty accurate. It's a risk problem, not an uncertainty one.

Innovation is different. By definition, tomorrow's breakthrough isn't predictable; if it was, someone probably would have come up with it today. Entrepreneurship is characterized by discontinuous jumps and surprising shifts.

If you doubt the challenge of forecasting the future, check out the 1989 film *Back to the Future II*. In this cult classic, Doc and Marty McFly travel twenty-five years into the future, ending up on October 21, 2015. When that moment actually came, fans of Michael J. Fox celebrated "Back to the Future Day" by looking at which technological predictions were proven right, and which ones didn't come through. *Back to the Future II* did predict the growth of videoconferencing, flat-panel screens, drones, wearables, and biometric identification. But no one has yet invented self-drying jackets, garbage-powered vehicles, and self-tying shoes. Most frustrating for the movie's die-hard fans, a well-functioning hoverboard remains elusive (though the movie was only one year out in predicting that the Chicago Cubs would break the Curse of the Billy Goat, with the team finally enjoying a World Series victory in 2016).

Just as interesting are the technologies that the moviemakers missed. They didn't anticipate the internet, smartphones, and massive data storage—which have together transformed the world of work and social interactions. There's no hint of the fall of the Soviet Union, the rise of China, an African American president, and the legalization of same-sex marriage in countries around the world.

The further ahead we try to predict, the harder the problem becomes. For the 1900 World Exhibition in Paris, a group of artists painted images of "France in the Year 2000."[3] Several pictures show people living with marine life (including one person traveling on a giant seahorse), but none depict space travel. The artists correctly forecast farming machines and helicopters, but wrongly predicted that police officers, postal workers, and firefighters would travel on personal planes, dodging the airships.

In short, overconfident futurologists would do well to check out "France in the Year 2000" and watch *Back to the Future II*. Both the exhibition and the movie are a reminder that anyone who is making plans ought to acknowledge uncertainty. As the old Danish proverb goes, it is difficult to make predictions, especially about the future.

But uncertainty doesn't mean we need to face the future naked and shivering. To encourage innovation, the United States should encourage healthy competition between research funders, foster moonshot innovation, and use prizes to encourage innovation. Policy makers should encourage permissionless markets, build catalytic networks and entrepreneurial ecosystems, consider variable patent terms, and support the use of public-sector and university science for innovation. Plus, beware of tax breaks and avoid extending copyright terms. And for good measure, update national statistics, so people know what's really going on in an increasingly digital economy.

On the equity side, the goal ought to be a set of institutions that provide a safety net—both for entrepreneurs who fall short of the stars and those left behind when the rocket takes off. It pays to think about such institutions as a form of insurance, providing greater resilience in the face of a changing world. If you're giving advice to a teenager, now is the time to tell them about the value of being flexible. Education isn't just an investment; it's about providing more life options.

To achieve this in the education system, we propose making teacher effectiveness the core focus of schooling policy, improving the quality of vocational training, simplifying the college loans system, and encouraging MOOCs. In the labor market, we propose instituting a US-wide ban on noncompete clauses, curbing the growth of occupational licensing, and creating a new employment category of independent workers. In the tax system, it would pay to raise the wage subsidy program known as the EITC. And it simply makes sense to use the talents of the 51 percent of the population who are women by encouraging technologies that make jobs more family friendly, and reforming laws that end up biasing the labor market against women. Gender equity isn't just worthwhile because it will boost productivity but also because—as Canadian Prime Minister Justin Trudeau might say—it's 2019.

As economist Sendhil Mullainathan puts it, "The safest prediction is that reality will outstrip our expectations. So, let us craft our policies not just for what we expect but for what will surely surprise us."[4] The task is to shape a future that looks more like *Star Trek* than *Terminator*.

Uncertainty need not be scary. The story of human history—particularly in recent centuries—is of how we have employed our shared ingenuity to improve lives. Longevity has risen. Whole diseases have been eliminated.

The typical job is more fulfilling and less painful. Entertainment is more abundant, and much of it is of higher quality (try spending a week watching television from a generation ago). Food standards have risen, and cars are safer than ever. Life is far from perfect, but there is a good deal to celebrate.

In Greek mythology, Prometheus was the brilliant hero who defied the gods by stealing fire and giving it to humanity. Yet it came at a cost, and he was punished cruelly by the gods for taking the risk that enabled human progress. For millennia, his name has been a byword for the dangers of questing for scientific knowledge—for the risks of going too far in pursuit of the secrets of the gods.

Today we need more Promethean innovators—willing to steal the secrets of the gods for the benefit of humanity. We should build a society that celebrates those who take risks for the betterment of our species.

But Prometheus didn't just bring fire. His name means "forethought": the capacity to plan for the future, not merely act on impulse.[5] A truly innovative society doesn't simply aim to "get rich quick." Spreading the benefits of innovation requires prudence as well as pluck. This means the economy must be adaptable and flexible as those new breakthroughs arrive. From children just starting school to older workers contemplating their next career move, governments can do more to maximize the benefits and minimize the costs. An entrepreneurial society need not be an unfair one. The goal is to be more innovative and more equal. Rather than an ominous "I'll be back" when it comes to the traditional innovation-equality trade-off, the motto should be "to boldly go" into a more productive and fairer future.

Notes

Chapter 1

1. Jerry Kaplan, Discussion with employees at Baidu, November 19, 2015, http://usa.baidu.com/jerry-kaplan-on-ai-robots-and-society-future-will-be-more-like-star-trek-than-terminator.

2. David Autor, "The Polarization of Job Opportunities in the U.S. Labor Market: Implications for Employment and Earnings," *Community Investments* 23, no. 2 (2011): 11–16.

3. Sara Hinkley, Annette Bernhardt, Sarah Thomason, *Race to the Bottom: How Low-Road Subcontracting Affects Working Conditions in California's Property Services Industry* (Berkeley, CA: UC Berkeley Labor Center, 2016).

4. Lawrence Mishel and Jessica Schieder, *CEO Compensation Surged in 2017* (Washington, DC: Economic Policy Institute, 2018).

5. Federal Reserve Economic Data, Series ID LREM25MAUSA156N (extracted November 22, 2018).

6. Federal Reserve Economic Data, Series ID LREM25FEUSA156N (extracted November 22, 2018).

7. Median real household income was just 2 percent higher in 2017 than in 1999. Kayla R. Fontenot, Jessica L. Semega, and Melissa A. Kollar, *Income and Poverty in the United States: 2017*, Current Population Reports, P60–263 (Washington, DC: Census Bureau, 2018), table A-2.

8. Real median male earnings for full-time, year-round workers were higher in 1973 than in 2017. Fontenot, Semega, and Kollar, *Income and Poverty*, table A-4.

9. From 1989 to 2017, real household incomes at the tenth percentile rose just 3 percent, compared with 30 percent at the ninetieth percentile. Fontenot, Semega, and Kollar, *Income and Poverty*, table A-2.

10. The overall poverty rate was 12.1 percent in 1969, and 12.3 percent in 2017. Fontenot, Semega, and Kollar, *Income and Poverty*, table B-1.

11. The poverty rate for all people aged under eighteen was 17.6 percent in 1966, and 17.5 percent in 2017. Fontenot, Semega, and Kollar, *Income and Poverty*, table B-2.

12. See, for example, the analysis of "total compensation: inequality, based on data from employers, in David H. Autor, Lawrence F. Katz, and Melissa S. Kearney, "Trends in US Wage Inequality: Revising the Revisionists," *Review of Economics and Statistics* 90, no. 2 (2008): 300–323.

13. "Time to Perk Up; Non-Wage Compensation in America," *The Economist* 429, no. 9117 (2018): 71.

14. The following results are drawn from Thomas Piketty, Emmanuel Saez, and Gabriel Zucman, "Distributional National Accounts: Methods and Estimates for the United States," *Quarterly Journal of Economics* 133, no. 2 (2017): 553–609.

15. *New Visionaries and the Chinese Century: Billionaires Insights 2018* (Zurich, Switzerland: UBS and PwC, 2018).

16. This comparison is presented in Piketty, Saez, and Zucman, "Distributional National Accounts."

17. Raj Chetty, David Grusky, Maximilian Hell, Nathaniel Hendren, Robert Manduca, and Jimmy Narang, "The Fading American Dream: Trends in Absolute Income Mobility Since 1940," *Science* 356, no. 6336 (2017): 398–406.

18. Emmanuel Saez and Gabriel Zucman, "Wealth Inequality in the United States since 1913: Evidence from Capitalized Income Tax Data," *Quarterly Journal of Economics* 131, no. 2 (2016): 519–578.

19. Sheelah Kolhatkar, "Dark Factory," *New Yorker*, October 23, 2017, 70–81.

20. Arthur M. Okun, *Equality and Efficiency: The Big Tradeoff* (Washington, DC: Brookings Institution, 1975).

21. "U.S. Federal Individual Income Tax Rates History, 1862–2013 (Nominal and Inflation-Adjusted Brackets)," Tax Foundation, October 17, 2013, https://taxfoundation.org/us-federal-individual-income-tax-rates-history-1913-2013-nominal-and-inflation-adjusted-brackets.

22. Nathan Rosenberg, "Uncertainty and Technological Change." In *Studies on Science and the Innovation Process: Selected Works of Nathan Rosenberg* (Singapore: World Scientific Publishing, 2010), 153–172.

23. Jonathan Morduch and Rachel Schneider, "Spikes and Dips: How Income Uncertainty Affects Households," U.S. Financial Diaries Project, Issue 1 (2013), www.usfinancialdiaries.org.

Chapter 2

1. "LiquiGlide Ketchup Bottle," https://www.youtube.com/watch?v=djwahGRi5iE.

2. Parmy Olson, "BlackBerry's Famous Last Words at 2007 iPhone Launch: 'We'll Be Fine,'" *Forbes*, May 26, 2015.

3. John Heilemann, "Reinventing the Wheel," *Time*, December 2, 2001.

4. Quoted in Tim Ferriss, *Tools of Titans: The Tactics, Routines, and Habits of Billionaires, Icons, and World-Class Performers* (Boston: Houghton, 2016), 174.

5. Gene, "Tesla Issues Software Update to Help Owners Flee Hurricane Irma by Increasing Battery Range," Teslarati, September 9, 2017, https://www.teslarati.com /tesla-issues-software-update-help-owners-flee-hurricane-irmas-evacuation-zone.

6. Marc Andreessen, "Why Software Is Eating the World," *Wall Street Journal*, August 20, 2011.

7. Paul Romer, "Economic Growth," October 12, 2015, https://paulromer.net /economic-growth.

8. Karl Rupp, "42 Years of Microprocessor Trend Data," February 15, 2018, www .karlrupp.net, with original data at github.com/karlrupp/microprocessor-trend-data.

9. Erik Brynjolfsson and Andrew McAfee, *The Second Machine Age: Work, Progress, and Prosperity in a Time of Brilliant Technologies* (New York: W. W. Norton, 2014).

10. These professors include Geoff Hinton (Toronto), Rich Sutton (Edmonton), and Yoshua Benigio (Montreal).

11. At least for lighter-skin men. For others, there is still some catching up to do.

12. "Frankenstein's Paperclips; Ethics," *The Economist* 419, no. 8995 (2016): 15.

13. "Finding a Voice," *The Economist* 422, no. 9022 (2017): 3.

14. "The Latest AI Can Work Things Out without Being Taught," *Economist*, October 21, 2017.

15. For more on this, see Ajay Agrawal, Joshua S. Gans, and Avi Goldfarb, *Prediction Machines: The Simple Economics of Artificial Intelligence* (Boston: Harvard Business Review Press, 2018).

16. Cade Metz and Steve Lohr, "IBM's New Program Would Like to Have a Debate with You," *New York Times*, June 20, 2018, B3.

17. Cade Metz, "This A.I. Can Build A.I. Itself," *New York Times*, November 6, 2017, B1.

18. Noam Scheiber, "A.I. Comes into Fashion," *New York Times*, July 8, 2018, BU1.

19. Iain Cockburn, Rebecca Henderson, and Scott Stern, "The Impact of Artificial Intelligence on Innovation: An Exploratory Analysis," in *The Economics of Artificial Intelligence: A Research Agenda*, ed. Ajay Agrawal, Joshua S. Gans, and Avi Goldfarb (Chicago: University of Chicago Press, 2019), 115–148.

20. Gordon makes another point too. Even if we see innovations of the same significance (the computer revolution and internet being a most recent set of examples), their contribution to economic progress can only be measured relative to the plethora of innovations diffused throughout the economy prior to 1973. By contrast, those inventions that emerged in the century up to 1973 brought about a change comparable to nothing before them.

21. Robert Solow, "We'd Better Watch Out," *New York Times Book Review*, July 12, 1987, 36.

22. David Dranove, Chris Forman, Avi Goldfarb, and Shane Greenstein, "The Trillion Dollar Conundrum: Complementarities and Health Information Technology," *American Economic Journal: Economic Policy* 6, no. 4 (2014): 239–270.

23. Benjamin F. Jones, "The Burden of Knowledge and the 'Death of the Renaissance Man': Is Innovation Getting Harder?," *Review of Economic Studies* 76, no. 1 (2009): 283–317. See also Patrick Collison and Michael Nielsen, "Science Is Getting Less Bang for the Buck," *Atlantic*, November 16, 2018.

24. Nicholas Bloom, Chad Jones, John Van Reenen, and Michael Webb, "Are Ideas Getting Harder to Find?," NBER Working Paper No. 23782 (Cambridge, MA: National Bureau of Economic Research, 2017).

25. Joel Mokyr, "The Next Stage of Invention," *City Journal* (Winter 2014): 1–20.

Chapter 3

1. Samuel Smiles, "Rev. William Lee, Inventor of the Socking Frame," Victorian Web, http://www.victorianweb.org/technology/inventors/lee.html.

2. The 1811 and 1821 British censuses asked about employment at a family level, so this figure likely underestimates the increase in the total number of jobs. See George Porter, *The Progress of the Nation in Its Various Social and Economical Relations from the Beginning of the Nineteenth Century* (London: John Murray, 1847), 52.

3. The story is recounted by Pliny the Elder and may be apocryphal.

4. Quoted in "Automation and Anxiety; the Impact on Jobs," *The Economist* 419, no. 8995 (2016): 10.

5. Quoted in Charlotte Curtis, "Machines vs. Workers," *New York Times*, February 8, 1983, C8.

6. Franklin Delano Roosevelt, State of the Union Address, January 3, 1940.

7. Greg Ip, "We Survived Spreadsheets, and We'll Survive AI," *Wall Street Journal*, August 2, 2017.

8. Steven Levy, "A Spreadsheet Way of Knowledge," Medium, October 24, 2014, https://medium.com/backchannel/a-spreadsheet-way-of-knowledge-8de60af7146e.

9. James Bessen, *Learning by Doing: The Real Connection between Innovation, Wages, and Wealth* (New Haven, CT: Yale University Press, 2015).

10. "Waymo Has Taken the Human out of Its Self-Driving Cars," *Wired*, November 7, 2017.

11. Tamra Johnson, "Think You're In Your Car More? You're Right. Americans Spend 70 Billion Hours Behind the Wheel," AAA NewsRoom, February 27, 2019.

12. Daniel Fagnant and Kara Kockelman, "Preparing a Nation for Autonomous Vehicles: Opportunities, Barriers, and Policy Recommendations," *Transportation Research Part A: Policy and Practice* 77 (2015): 167–181.

13. "A Different World; Society," *The Economist* 426, no. 9081 (2018): 11.

14. Laurel Hamers, "Five Challenges for Self-Driving Cars," *ScienceNews*, December 12, 2016.

15. Edmond Awad, Sohan Dsouza, Richard Kim, Jonathan Schulz, Joseph Henrich, Azim Shariff, Jean-François Bonnefon, and Iyad Rahwan, "The Moral Machine Experiment," *Nature* 563, no. 7729 (2018): 59–64.

16. Quoted in "Whom Should Self-Driving Cars Protect in an Accident?," *Economist*, October 27, 2018.s

17. Hamers, "Five Challenges for Self-Driving Cars."

18. "Reinventing Wheels; Autonomous Vehicles," *The Economist* 426, no. 9081 (2018): 4.

19. Alexis C. Madrigal, "Could Self-Driving Trucks be Good for Truckers?," *Atlantic*, February 1, 2018.

20. Donald M. Fisk, "American Labor in the 20th Century," *Compensation and Working Conditions* (Fall 2001), https://www.bls.gov/opub/mlr/cwc/american-labor-in-the-20th-century.pdf.

21. These examples are drawn from "The Human Cumulus; Digital Labour," *The Economist* 424, no. 9055 (2017): 55.

22. Robyn Caplan, *Content or Context Moderation? Artisanal, Community-Reliant, and Industrial Approaches* (New York: Data and Society Research Institute, 2018).

23. Atul Gawande, "The Upgrade," *New Yorker*, November 12, 2018, 62–73.

24. Greg Ip, "Workers: Fear Not the Robot Apocalypse," *Wall Street Journal*, September 5, 2017.

25. James Bloodworth, *Hired: Six Months Undercover in Low-Wage Britain* (London: Atlantic Books, 2018).

26. Gill Pratt, "Is a Cambrian Explosion Coming for Robotics?," *Journal of Economic Perspectives* 29, no. 3 (2015): 51–60.

27. Bill Snyder, "Bill Gates, Stephen Hawking Say Artificial Intelligence Represents Real Threat," *CIO*, January 30, 2015.

28. "Nick Bostrom on Superintelligence," EconTalk, December 1, 2014, http://www.econtalk.org/nick-bostrom-on-superintelligence.

29. Joshua S. Gans, "Self-Regulating Artificial General Intelligence," Rotman School of Management Working Paper No. 3124512, February 15, 2018, https://ssrn.com/abstract=3124512.

30. Charles Stross, *Accelerando* (New York: ACE Hardcover, 2005), 250.

31. Stross, *Accelerando*, 316.

32. Stuart Armstrong, "How We're Predicting AI" (paper presented at the Singularity Summit, San Francisco, October 13–14, 2012).

33. David Ricardo, *On the Principles of Political Economy and Taxation*, 3rd ed. (London: Murray, 1821). See also Paul A. Samuelson, "Mathematical Vindication of Ricardo on Machinery," *Journal of Political Economy* 96, no. 2 (1988): 274–282.

34. Wassily Leontief, "National Perspective: The Definition of Problem and Opportunity," in *The Long-Term Impact of Technology on Employment and Unemployment: A National Academy of Engineering Symposium, June 30, 1983* (Washington, DC: National Academy Press, 1983), 3.

35. Steve Henn, "Robots Are Really Bad at Folding Towels," *Planet Money*, May 19, 2015, http://www.npr.org/sections/money/2015/05/19/407736307/robots-are-really-bad-at-folding-towels.

36. Tuan Mai, "Not the Greatest Idea Ever: The Robot Barber," Tom's Guide, April 7, 2012, http://www.tomsguide.com/us/Robot-Barber-Haircut,news-14578.html.

37. Cade Metz, "A.I. Researchers Leave Elon Musk Lab to Begin Robotics Start-up," *New York Times*, November 7, 2017, B1.

38. David H. Autor, Frank Levy, and Richard J. Murnane, "The Skill Content of Recent Technological Change: An Empirical Exploration," *Quarterly Journal of Economics* (2003): 1279–1333.

39. David H. Autor, "Why Are There Still So Many Jobs? The History and Future of Workplace Automation," *Journal of Economic Perspectives* 29, no. 3 (2015): 3–30.

40. Maarten Goos, Alan Manning, and Anna Salomons, "Explaining Job Polarization: Routine-Biased Technological Change and Offshoring," *American Economic Review* 104, no. 8 (2014): 2509–2526.

41. International Federation of Robotics, *World Robotics 2016 Industrial Robots* (Frankfurt: International Federation of Robotics, 2016).

42. Daron Acemoglu and Pascual Restrepo, "Robots and Jobs: Evidence from US Labor Markets," NBER Working Paper No. 23285 (Cambridge, MA: National Bureau of Economic Research, 2017).

43. Anders Akerman, Ingvil Gaarder, and Magne Mogstad, "The Skill Complementarity of Broadband Internet," *Quarterly Journal of Economics* 130, no. 4 (2015): 1781–1824.

44. "Renaissance; Surgery," *The Economist* 425, no. 9067 (2017): 67.

45. Eric Wills, "Right out of the Box," *Australian Financial Review*, November 13, 2015, 4R–5R.

46. Xavier Gabaix and Augustin Landier, "Why Has CEO Pay Increased So Much?," *Quarterly Journal of Economics* 123, no. 1 (2008): 49–100.

47. See Gerald Mayer, "Union Membership Trends in the United States," Congressional Research Service, Washington, DC, 2004; Barry T. Hirsch and David A. Macpherson, "Union Membership and Coverage Database from the Current Population Survey: Note," *Industrial and Labor Relations Review* 56, no. 2 (January 2003): 349–354, updated at http://unionstats.gsu.edu/All-Wage-and-Salary-Workers.htm.

48. Lawrence Mishel, "Unions, Inequality, and Faltering Middle-Class Wages," Issue Brief No. 342, Economic Policy Institute, Washington, DC, 2012.

49. Daron Acemoglu, Philippe Aghion, and Giovanni L. Violante, "Deunionization, Technical Change, and Inequality," *Carnegie-Rochester Conference Series on Public Policy* 55, no. 1 (December 2001): 229–264.

50. In February 1968, the federal minimum wage was $1.60, which has the same buying power as $11.79 today (adjusted using the consumer price index for all urban consumers).

51. For a discussion of this issue, see Anthony B. Atkinson and Andrew Leigh, "The Distribution of Top Incomes in Five Anglo-Saxon Countries over the Long Run," *Economic Record* 89, no. S1 (2013): 31–47.

52. Paul R. Krugman, "Trade and Wages, Reconsidered," *Brookings Papers on Economic Activity*, 39, no. 1 (Spring 2008): 103–154.

53. Krugman, "Trade and Wages, Reconsidered."

54. US Census Bureau, "Top Trading Partners—Total Trade, Exports, Imports," Foreign Trade Statistics, December 2007, https://www.census.gov/foreign-trade/statistics/highlights/top/top0712.html.

55. David H. Autor, David Dorn, and Gordon H. Hanson, "The China Syndrome: Local Labor Market Effects of Import Competition in the United States," *American Economic Review* 103, no. 6 (2013): 2121–2168. See also David H. Autor, David Dorn, and Gordon H. Hanson, "The China Shock: Learning from Labor-Market Adjustment to Large Changes in Trade," *Annual Review of Economics* 8, no. 1 (2016): 205–240.

56. David H. Autor, "Did China Eat America's Jobs?," interview by Stephen J. Dubner, Freakonomics Radio, January 25, 2017, http://freakonomics.com/podcast/china-eat-americas-jobs.

57. Adam Bluestein, "The Most Entrepreneurial Group in America Wasn't Born in America," *Inc.*, February 2015.

58. See, for example, Rachel Friedberg and Jennifer Hunt, "The Impact of Immigrants on Host Country Wages, Employment and Growth," *Journal of Economic Perspectives* 9, no. 2 (Spring 1995): 23–44.

59. See George J. Borjas, "The Labor Demand Curve Is Downward Sloping: Reexamining the Impact of Immigration on the Labor Market," *Quarterly Journal of Economics* 118, no. 4 (November 2003): 1335–1374.

60. William R. Kerr, *The Gift of Global Talent: How Migration Shapes Business, Economy, and Society* (Stanford, CA: Stanford University Press, 2018).

61. Stuart Anderson, *Immigrants and Billion Dollar Startups*, National Foundation for American Policy, Arlington, VA, March 2016, https://www.immigrationresearch-info.org/system/files/Immigrants-and-Billion-Dollar-Startups.NFAP-Policy-Brief.March-2016.pdf. See also Farhad Manjoo, "Why Silicon Valley Wouldn't Work without Immigrants," *New York Times*, February 9, 2017, B1.

62. Kerr, *Gift of Global Talent*.

63. Andrea Morrison, Sergio Petralia, and Dario Diodato, "Migration and Invention in the Age of Mass Migration," Papers in Evolutionary Economic Geography no. 18.35, Utrecht University, Department of Human Geography and Spatial Planning, Group Economic Geography, October 2018.

64. This observation is attributed to Brink Lindsey, quoted in "Philip Auerswald on the Rise of Populism," *EconTalk*, September 25, 2017, http://www.econtalk.org/archives/2017/09/philip_auerswal.html. For data, see US Bureau of Labor Statistics, *All Employees: Manufacturing [MANEMP]*, FRED, Federal Reserve Bank of Saint Louis, February 16, 2019, https://fred.stlouisfed.org/series/MANEMP; Erin Lett and Judith Banister, "China's Manufacturing Employment and Compensation Costs: 2002–06,"

Monthly Labor Review, April 2009, https://stats.bls.gov/opub/mlr/2009/04/art3full
.pdf.

65. Quoted in Claire Miller, "What's Really Killing Jobs? It's Automation, Not
China," *New York Times*, December 22, 2016, A3.

66. Carl Benedikt Frey and Michael A. Osborne, "The Future of Employment: How
Susceptible Are Jobs to Computerisation?," *Technological Forecasting and Social
Change* 114 (2017): 254–280.

67. This critique draws on Jeff Borland and Michael Coelli, "Are Robots Taking Our
Jobs?," *Australian Economic Review* 50, no. 4 (2017): 377–397.

68. Ed Felten, Manav Rai, and Robert Seamans, "A Method to Link Advances in Artificial Intelligence to Occupational Abilities," *American Economic Association Papers
and Proceedings* 108 (May 2018): 55–57.

69. Daron Acemoglu and Pascual Restrepo, "The Race between Machine and Man:
Implications of Technology for Growth, Factor Shares, and Employment," National
Bureau of Economic Research Working Paper No. 22252 (Cambridge, MA: National
Bureau of Economic Research, 2016).

70. US Bureau of Labor Statistics, Employment Projections, Occupations, tables 1.3
and 1.5, last modified April 11, 2018, https://www.bls.gov/emp/tables.htm.

71. Richard Freeman, "Is a Great Labor Shortage Coming? Replacement Demand in
the Global Economy," in *Reshaping the American Workforce in a Changing Economy*,
ed. Harry J. Holzer and Demetra Nightingale (Washington, DC, Urban Institute
Press, 2007): 3–24.

Chapter 4

1. Bureau of Labor Statistics, US Department of Labor, "Physical Strength Required
for Jobs in Different Occupations in 2016," *Economics Daily*, April 10, 2017, http://
www.bls.gov/opub/ted/2017/physical-strength-required-for-jobs-in-different
-occupations-in-2016.htm.

2. Ruth Alexander, "Where Are You on the Global Pay Scale?," BBC News, March
29, 2012, https://www.bbc.com/news/magazine-17543356.

3. William Larson, "New Estimates of Value of Land of the United States," Bureau of
Economic Analysis, US Department of Commerce, April 2015.

4. See GivingPledge.org.

5. Felix Salmon, "Krugman vs Summers: The Debate," *Reuters*, November 15, 2011.

6. Paul Graham, "Economic Inequality," January 2016, http://www.paulgraham.com
/ineq.html.

7. Graham, "Economic Inequality."

8. These were the respective occupations of Zuckerberg's and Jobs's fathers.

9. This is because the trader's cumulative salary of $500,000 is 1/2000th of the $1 billion company created by a successful entrepreneur.

10. Ignoring the tax-free threshold, a 30 percent tax rate on traders and entrepreneurs means that the trader's cumulative after-tax salary of $350,000 is 1/2000th of the successful entrepreneur's $700 million after-tax earnings.

11. Bill Retherford, "How Many Exoplanets Might Have Life? The Number Is … ," *Forbes*, May 28, 2018.

12. Ignoring the tax-free threshold, a 0 percent tax rate on traders and 30 percent tax rate on entrepreneurs means that the trader's cumulative untaxed salary of $500,000 is 1/1400th of the successful entrepreneur's $700 million after-tax earnings.

13. Ignoring the tax-free threshold, a 30 percent tax rate on traders and 0 percent tax rate on entrepreneurs means that the trader's cumulative after-tax salary of $350,000 is 1/2857th of the successful entrepreneur's $1 billion untaxed earnings.

14. Ufuk Akcigit, John Grigsby, Tom Nicholas, and Stefanie Stantcheva, "Taxation and Innovation in the 20th Century," NBER Working Paper No. 24982 (Cambridge, MA: National Bureau of Economic Research, 2018).

15. This is based on our analysis of the Organisation for Economic Co-operation and Development's patent statistics for the United States in 1999–2013 (all available years in that data set at the time of this writing).

16. National Science Board, *Science and Engineering Indicators 2018*, NSB-2018–1. National Science Foundation, Alexandria, VA, 2018, 8–13.

17. Enrico Moretti and Daniel Wilson, "The Effect of State Taxes on the Geographical Location of Top Earners: Evidence from Star Scientists," *American Economic Review* 107, no. 7 (2017): 1858–1903.

18. Recent research points out that exposing talented youngsters to innovation is likely to draw in more star innovators than changing income tax rates: Alexander M. Bell, Raj Chetty, Xavier Jaravel, Neviana Petkova, and John Van Reenen, "Do Tax Cuts Produce More Einsteins? The Impacts of Financial Incentives Versus Exposure to Innovation on the Supply of Inventors," *Journal of the European Economic Association* (forthcoming).

19. Rachel Griffith, Helen Miller, and Martin, O'Connell, "Corporate Taxes and Intellectual Property: Simulating the Effect of Patent Boxes," IFS Briefing Note 112, January 14, 2011; Annette Alstadsæter, Salvador Barrios, Gaetan Nicodeme, Agnieszka Maria Skonieczna, and Antonio Vezzani, "Patent Boxes Design, Patents Location, and Local R&D," *Economic Policy* 33, no. 93 (January 2018): 131–177;

Fabian Gaessler, Bronwyn Hall, and Dietmar Harhoff, "Should There Be Lower Taxes on Patent Income?," NBER Working Paper No. 24843 (Cambridge, MA: National Bureau of Economic Research, 2018). See also Gaéten de Rassenfosse, *Patent Box Policies* (report prepared for the Office of the Chief Economist, Department of Industry, Innovation and Science, Canberra, Australia, November 2015).

20. Barack Obama, "The Way Ahead," *The Economist* 421, no. 9010 (2016): 22.

21. Pian Shu, "Innovating in Science and Engineering or 'Cashing In' on Wall Street? Evidence on Elite STEM Talent," Harvard Business School Working Paper No. 16–067, Boston, 2016.

22. N. Gregory Mankiw, "Defending the One Percent," *Journal of Economic Perspectives* 27, no. 3 (Summer 2013): 21–34.

23. Ken Cavalluzzo and John Wolken, "Small Business Loan Turndowns, Personal Wealth, and Discrimination." *Journal of Business* 78, no. 6 (2005): 2153–2178; Naranchimeg Mijid and Alexandra Bernasek, "Gender and the Credit Rationing of Small Businesses," *Social Science Journal* 50, no. 1 (2013): 55–65.

24. Tyler Cowen, "Equality Is a Mediocre Goal. Aim for Progress," *Bloomberg*, May 1, 2018.

Chapter 5

1. Rebecca Solnit, "Diary," *London Review of Books* 35, no. 3 (February 7, 2013): 34–35.

2. Rory Carroll, "Oakland: The City That Told Google to Get Lost," *Guardian*, February 11, 2014.

3. Manhattan rents from https://www.rentcafe.com/average-rent-market-trends/us/ny/manhattan.

4. The average disposable income per capita was $39,500 in February 2018. US Bureau of Economic Analysis, "Real Disposable Income: Per Capita (A229RX0)," FRED, Federal Reserve Bank of Saint Louis, December 21, 2018, https://fred.stlouisfed.org/series/A229RX0.

5. Richard Florida, *The New Urban Crisis: How Our Cities Are Increasing Inequality, Deepening Segregation, and Failing the Middle Class—and What We Can Do About It* (New York: Basic Books, 2017), 48.

6. Chris McCann, "1979 to 2015—Average Rent in San Francisco," *Medium*, August 17, 2015, https://medium.com/@mccannatron/1979-to-2015-average-rent-in-san-francisco-33aaea22de0e.

7. Carroll, "Oakland."

8. Tom Perkins, "Progressive Kristallnacht Coming?," *Wall Street Journal*, January 24, 2014.

9. For a history, see Randall Stross, *The Launchpad: Inside Y Combinator* (New York: Portfolio, 2012).

10. Paul Graham, "Economic Inequality," January 2016, http://www.paulgraham.com/ineq.html.

11. Jorge Guzman and Scott Stern, "Where Is Silicon Valley," *Science* 347, no. 6222 (February 6, 2015): 606–609.

12. Astrid Marinoni, "Entrepreneurship and Inequality," *Academy of Management Proceedings*, no. 1 (2017): 11937.

13. Based on StatCounter, "Search Engine Market Share in United States of America," March 2019, http://gs.statcounter.com/search-engine-market-share/all/united-states-of-america.

14. National Academies of Sciences, Engineering, and Medicine, *Information Technology and the U.S. Workforce: Where Are We and Where Do We Go from Here?* (Washington, DC: National Academies Press, 2017), 91.

15. National Academies of Sciences, Engineering, and Medicine, *Information Technology and the U.S. Workforce*, 91.

16. Mohsen Mohaghegh, "Evolution of Inequality in the U.S. Entrepreneurial Activity and Financial Intermediation," (working paper, Ohio State University, Columbus, 2018).

17. "M&A Statistics," Institute for Mergers, Acquisitions, and Alliances, https://imaa-institute.org/mergers-and-acquisitions-statistics.

18. Dan Andrews, Chiara Criscuolo, and Peter N. Gal, "The Global Productivity Slowdown, Technology Divergence, and Public Policy: A Firm Level Perspective," Hutchins Center Working Paper No. 24, Brookings Institution, 2016.

19. David H. Autor, David Dorn, Lawrence F. Katz, Christina Patterson, and John Van Reenen, "Concentrating on the Fall of the Labor Share," *American Economic Review* 107, no. 5 (2017): 180–185.

20. Research by McKinsey Solutions and the Council of Economic Advisers, cited in "A Lapse in Concentration; Deregulation and Competition," *The Economist* 421, no. 9009 (2016): 14.

21. Simcha Barkai, "Declining Labor and Capital Shares" (working paper, London Business School, 2017).

22. Joshua S. Gans, Andrew Leigh, Martin Schmalz, and Adam Triggs, "Inequality and Market Concentration, When Shareholding Is More Skewed Than Consumption,"

Oxford Review of Economic Policy (forthcoming). See also Sean F. Ennis, Pedro Gonzaga, and Chris Pike, "Inequality: A Hidden Cost of Market Power," *Oxford Review of Economic Policy* (forthcoming).

23. Anita Wölfl, Isabelle Wanner, Oliver Roehn, and Giuseppe Nicoletti, "Product Market Regulation: Extending the Analysis beyond OECD Countries," Economics Department Working Paper No. 799 (Paris: OECD Publishing, October 6, 2010).

24. Sean F. Ennis, "Commerce Affected by Cross-Border Private Cartels," OECD Working Paper No. 3 (Paris: OECD Publishing, 2014).

25. Jae Song, David J. Price, Fatih Guvenen, Nicholas Bloom, and Till Von Wachter, "Firming Up Inequality," *Quarterly Journal of Economics* 134, no. 1 (2019): 1–50.

26. Erling Barth, Alex Bryson, James C. Davis, and Richard Freeman, "It's Where You Work: Increases in the Dispersion of Earnings across Establishments and Individuals in the U.S.," *Journal of Labor Economics* 34, no. S2 (April 2016): S67–S97.

27. "Lapse in Concentration."

28. Gene M. Grossman, Elhanan Helpman, Ezra Oberfield, and Thomas Sampson, "The Productivity Slowdown and the Declining Labor Share: A Neoclassical Exploration," NBER Working Paper No. 23853 (Cambridge, MA: National Bureau of Economic Research, 2017), 2. See also Barkai, "Declining Labor and Capital Shares."

29. Loukas Karabarbounis and Brent Neiman, "The Global Decline of the Labor Share," *Quarterly Journal of Economics* 129, no. 1 (2013): 61–103; David H. Autor, David Dorn, Lawrence F. Katz, Christina Patterson, and John Van Reenen, "The Fall of the Labor Share and the Rise of Superstar Firms," NBER Working Paper No. 23396 (Cambridge, MA: National Bureau of Economic Research, 2017).

30. Gene M. Grossman, Elhanan Helpman, Ezra Oberfield, and Thomas Sampson, "The Productivity Slowdown and the Declining Labor Share: A Neoclassical Exploration," NBER Working Paper No. 23853 (Cambridge, MA: National Bureau of Economic Research, 2017), 3.

31. Autor, Dorn, Katz, Patterson, and Van Reenen, "Fall of the Labor Share and the Rise of Superstar Firms."

32. Autor, Dorn, Katz, Patterson, and Van Reenen, "Fall of the Labor Share and the Rise of Superstar Firms."

33. Anders Akerman, Edwin Leuven, and Magne Mogstad, "Information Frictions, Broadband Internet, and the Relationship between Distance and Trade" (working paper, University of Chicago, 2017).

34. See Jonathan Tepper and Denise Hearn, *The Myth of Capitalism: Monopolies and the Death of Competition* (New York: Wiley, 2018).

35. John C. Bogle, "The First Index Mutual Fund: A History of Vanguard Index Trust and the Vanguard Index Strategy," Bogle Financial Markets Research Center, https://www.vanguard.com/bogle_site/lib/sp19970401.html.

36. Allan Roth, "Can Indexing Become Too Big?," AARP, May 27, 2015, http://blog.aarp.org/2015/05/27/can-indexing-become-too-big.

37. Rachel Evans, Dani Burger, and Sabrina Willmer, "The Passive War," *Bloomberg Markets*, June 5, 2017, 62–69.

38. Jan Fichtner, Eelke M. Heemskerk, and Javier Garcia-Bernardo, "Hidden Power of the Big Three? Passive Index Funds, Re-Concentration of Corporate Ownership, and New Financial Risk," *Business and Politics* 19, no. 2 (2017): 1–29.

39. José Azar, Martin C. Schmalz, and Isabel Tecu, "Anticompetitive Effects of Common Ownership," *Journal of Finance* 73, no. 4 (2018): 1513–1565.

40. José Azar, Sahil Raina, and Martin C. Schmalz, "Ultimate Ownership and Bank Competition" (working paper, University of Michigan, Ann Arbor, 2016).

41. Philippe Aghion, Ufuk Akcigit, Antonin Bergeaud, Richard Blundell, and David Hémous, "Innovation and Top Income Inequality," *Review of Economic Studies* 86, no. 1 (2019): 1–45.

Chapter 6

1. Atul Gawande, "The Score: The Effort to Make Childbirth Safer," *New Yorker*, October 9, 2006, 58–67.

2. Gawande, "The Score."

3. Walter Radcliffe, *The Secret Instrument: The Birth of the Midwifery Forceps* (New York: William Heinemann Medical Books, 1947).

4. Another example in which secrecy was used was in early cures for tuberculosis: John Farey, "Secrets Specific for Scrofula," from *Minutes of Evidence before Select Committee of the House of Commons on the Law Relative to Patents for Inventions* (House of Commons, London, 1829).

5. For more details on this story, see John Seabrook, "The Flash of Genius," *New Yorker*, January 11, 1993, 38–52.

6. Joshua S. Gans, David Hsu, and Scott Stern, "When Does Start-Up Innovation Spur the Gale of Creative Destruction?," *RAND Journal of Economics* 33, no. 4 (2002): 571–586.

7. Joshua S. Gans and Scott Stern, "Is There a Market for Ideas?," *Industrial and Corporate Change* 19, no. 3 (2010): 805–837.

8. Rodney H. Metts and Barry D. Thomas, "Clock for Keeping Time at a Rate Other Than Human Time," U.S. Patent No. 5,023,850, June 11, 1991.

9. Jane Wells, "Mom's Constipation Turns into a $30 Million Cult Juggernaut," *Make It*, CNBC, August 23, 2016, https://www.cnbc.com/2016/08/23/moms-constipation -turns-into-30-million-cult-juggernaut.html.

10. Petra Moser, "Patents and Innovation: Evidence from Economic History," *Journal of Economic Perspectives* 27, no. 1 (2013): 23–44.

11. Alexander Tabarrok, "Innovation Policy and Australia," February 2013, https:// grattan.edu.au/wp-content/uploads/2014/05/908_tabarrok_alliance_21.pdf.

12. Adam Jaffe and Josh Lerner, *Innovation and Its Discontents: How Our Broken Patent System Is Endangering Innovation and Progress, and What to Do about It* (Princeton, NJ: Princeton University Press, 2004).

13. Jacob Kastrenakes, "Qualcomm Must License Patents to Competing Chipmakers, Court Rules," *'Verge*, November 6, 2018, https://www.theverge.com/2018/11/6 /18069602/qualcomm-ftc-lawsuit-patent-licensing-frand.

14. Max Chafkin and Ian King, "Apple and Qualcomm's Billion-Dollar War over an $18 Part," *Bloomberg*, October 4, 2017.

15. This is the standard patent duration, covering "utility patents" filed since 1995. Design patents (for decorative, nonfunctional products) have a fifteen-year duration.

16. Adam Thierer, *Permissionless Innovation: The Continuing Case for Comprehensive Technological Freedom* (Arlington, VA: Mercatus Center at George Mason University, 2016).

17. Hans K. Hvide and Benjamin F. Jones, "University Innovation and the Professor's Privilege," *American Economic Review* 108, no. 7 (2018): 1860–1898.

18. Mark Clark, "Suppressing Innovation: Bell Laboratories and Magnetic Recording," *Technology and Culture* 34, no. 3 (1993): 516–538.

19. Clark, "Suppressing Innovation," 534.

20. Joshua S. Gans, "Weak versus Strong Net Neutrality," *Journal of Regulatory Economics* 47, no. 2 (2015): 183–200.

21. See Joshua S. Gans, "Enhancing Competition with Data and Identity Portability," Hamilton Project, Brookings Institution, 2018, https://www.brookings.edu /research/enhancing-competition-with-data-and-identity-portability.

22. See Luigi Zingales and Guy Rolnik, "A Way to Own Your Social-Media Data," *New York Times*, June 30, 2017, A23.

23. Mariana Mazzucato, *The Entrepreneurial State: Debunking Public vs. Private Sector Myths* (London: Anthem Press, 2013).

24. Ekaterina Galkina Cleary, Jennifer M. Beierlein, Navleen Surjit Khanuja, Laura M. McNamee, and Fred D. Ledley, "Contribution of NIH Funding to New Drug Approvals 2010–2016," *PNAS* 115, no 10 (2018): 2329–2334.

25. Quoted in Rana Foroohar, "Why Hillary Clinton Is Right about Pfizer," *Time*, November 24, 2015.

26. Fred L. Block and Matthew R. Keller, *State of Innovation: The U.S. Government's Role in Technology Development* (New York, Routledge, 2015).

27. Fred L. Block, "Seeing the State: In Search of a New History of Economic Modernity," *Breakthrough* (Number 9, Summer 2018), https://thebreakthrough.org/journal/no.-9-summer-2018/seeing-the-state.

28. Ajay Agrawal, Alberto Galasso, and Alexander Oettl, "Roads and Innovation," *Review of Economics and Statistics* 99, no. 2 (July 2017): 417–434.

29. Shai Bernstein, Xavier Giroud, and Richard R. Townsend, "The Impact of Venture Capital Monitoring," *Journal of Finance* 71, no. 4 (2016): 1591–1622.

30. Elizabeth Lyons and Laurina Zhang, "The Impact of Entrepreneurship Programs on Minorities," *American Economic Review* 107, no. 5 (2017): 303–307.

31. Friedman made the point in reverse, but the equality holds both ways.

32. Anatole France, *Le Lys Rouge* (Paris: Calmann-Lévy, 1894), 118.

33. Philippe Aghion, Ufuk Akcigit, Ari Hyytinen, and Otto Toivanen, "The Social Origins of Inventors," NBER Working Paper No. 24110 (Cambridge, MA: National Bureau of Economic Research, 2017).

34. Alexander M. Bell, Raj Chetty, Xavier Jaravel, Neviana Petkova, and John Van Reenen, "Who Becomes an Inventor in America? The Importance of Exposure to Innovation," *Quarterly Journal of Economics* 134, no. 2 (2019): 647–713.

35. Ufuk Akcigit, John Grigsby, and Tom Nicholas, "The Rise of American Ingenuity: Innovation and Inventors of the Golden Age," NBER Working Paper No. 23047 (Cambridge, MA: National Bureau of Economic Research, 2017).

36. Malcolm Gladwell, *Outliers: The Story of Success* (New York: Little, Brown and Company, 2008), 51.

37. Bell, Chetty, Jaravel, Petkova, and Van Reenen, "Who Becomes an Inventor in America?"

38. Lene Foss and Colette Henry, "Doing Gender in Innovation: A Thematic Review and Critique of the Literature," in *Research Handbook on Gender and Innovation*, ed. Gry A. Alsos, Ulla Hytti, and Elisabet Ljunggren (Cheltenham, UK: Edward Elgar, 2016), 17–50.

39. Agrawal, Galasso, and Oettl, "Roads and Innovation," 417–434.

40. Jorge Guzman and Scott Stern, "Where Is Silicon Valley?," *Science* 347, no. 6222 (February 6, 2015): 606–609.

41. To borrow a phrase from Kevin Rivette and David Kline, *Rembrandts in the Attic: Unlocking the Hidden Value of Patents* (Cambridge, MA: Harvard Business Review Press, 1999).

42. Jorge Guzman, "Go West Young Firm: Agglomeration and Embeddedness in Startup Migrations to Silicon Valley," Columbia Business School Research Paper No. 18–49 (New York: Columbia University, 2018).

43. Hans Hvide and Paul Oyer, "Dinner Table Human Capital and Entrepreneurship," NBER Working Paper No. 24198 (Cambridge, MA: National Bureau of Economic Research, 2018).

44. Ajay Agrawal and Iain Cockburn, "The Anchor Tenant Hypothesis: Exploring the Role of Large, Local, R&D-Intensive Firms in Regional Innovation Systems," *International Journal of Industrial Organization* 21, no. 9 (2003): 1227–1253.

45. Research at the Creative Destruction Lab backs up this finding. See Kevin A. Bryan, András Tilcsik, and Brooklyn Zhu, "Which Entrepreneurs Are Coachable, and Why?," *American Economic Review Papers and Proceedings* 107, no. 5 (2017): 312–316.

46. Brian A. Jacob and Lars Lefgren, "The Impact of Research Grant Funding on Scientific Productivity," *Journal of Public Economics* 95, no. 9 (2011): 1168–1177; Jason Gush, Adam B. Jaffe, Victoria Larsen, and Athene Laws, "The Effect of Public Funding on Research Output: The New Zealand Marsden Fund," *New Zealand Economic Papers* 52, no. 2 (2018): 227–248.

47. Ashish Arora and Alfonso Gambardella, "The Impact of NSF Support for Basic Research in Economics," *Annales d'Économie et de Statistique* 79–80 (July 2005): 91–117.

48. Pierre Azoulay, Joshua S. Graff Zivin, and Gustavo Manso, "Incentives and Creativity: Evidence from the Academic Life Sciences," *RAND Journal of Economics* 42, no. 3 (2011): 527–554.

49. Alexander Tabarrok, "Patent Theory versus Patent Law," *B.E. Journal of Economic Analysis and Policy* 1, no. 1 (2002): 1–26.

50. For a useful review of ten countries' innovation strategy documents, see Isaac Stanley, Alex Glennie, and Madeleine Gabriel, "How Inclusive Is Innovation Policy? Insights from an International Comparison" (working paper, Nesta, London, 2018).

51. Gavi, the Vaccine Alliance and the World Bank, "Creating Markets to Save Lives," Advance Market Commitments for Vaccines, Geneva, Switzerland, http://www.leadinggroup.org/IMG/pdf/AMC_factsheet_1_.pdf.

52. The idea was originally proposed in Ruth Levine, Michael Kremer, and Alice Albright, *Making Markets for Vaccines: Ideas to Action*, report of the Center for Global Development Advance Market Commitment Working Group, 2005, https://www.cgdev.org/sites/default/files/archive/doc/books/vaccine/MakingMarkets-complete.pdf.

53. "Measuring Tax Support for R&D and Innovation," OECD, http://www.oecd.org/sti/rd-tax-stats.htm.

54. Silvia Appelt, Matej Bajgar, Chiara Criscuolo, and Fernando Galindo-Rueda, "R&D Tax Incentives: Evidence on Design, Incidence, and Impacts," OECD Science, Technology, and Industry Policy Papers No. 32 (Paris, OECD Publishing, 2016), 8.

55. Jonathan Haskel and Stian Westlake, *Capitalism without Capital: The Rise of the Intangible Economy* (Princeton, NJ: Princeton University Press, 2017).

56. Tim Harford, *Fifty Things That Made the Modern Economy* (London: Little, Brown and Company, 2017).

Chapter 7

1. Nick Wingfield, "Unboxing Amazon's Ambitions," *New York Times*, March 26, 2017, BU1.

2. "Jeff Bezos, Amazon and the Final Frontier," In the Black, November 1, 2017, https://www.intheblack.com/articles/2017/11/01/amazon-power-invention.

3. Jong-Wha Lee and Hanol Lee, "Human Capital in the Long Run," *Journal of Development Economics* 122 (September 2016): 147–169.

4. Forty-six percent of high school graduates enroll in a four-year college: "Economic News Release," Bureau of Labor Statistics, US Department of Labor, April 26, 2018, https://www.bls.gov/news.release/hsgec.t01.htm. Fifty-nine percent who enroll in a four-year degree program graduate within six years: "Fast Facts," National Center for Education Statistics, https://nces.ed.gov/fastfacts/display.asp?id=40.

5. The most recent long-term trends report is for 2012. See Nation's Report Card, *Trends in Academic Progress 2012* (Washington, DC: National Center for Education Statistics, US Department of Education, 2013).

6. On demographic trends and "Simpson's paradox," see Chad Aldeman, "Over the Long Term, NAEP Scores Are Way, Way Up," Education Next, October 26, 2015, http://educationnext.org/over-the-long-term-naep-scores-are-way-way-up.

7. Stephen Provasnik, Lydia Malley, Maria Stephens, Katherine Landeros, Robert Perkins, and Judy H. Tang, *Highlights from TIMSS and TIMSS Advanced 2015* (Washington, DC: National Center for Education Statistics, US Department of Education, 2016).

8. David Kastberg, Jessica Ying Chan, Gordon Murray, and Patrick Gonzales, *Performance of U.S. 15-Year-Old Students in Science, Reading, and Mathematics Literacy in an*

International Context (Washington, DC: National Center for Education Statistics, US Department of Education, 2015).

9. Sean P. Corcoran, William N. Evans, and Robert M. Schwab, "Women, the Labor Market, and the Declining Relative Quality of Teachers," *Journal of Policy Analysis and Management* 23, no. 3 (2004): 449–470; Sean P. Corcoran, "Long-Run Trends in the Quality of Teachers: Evidence and Implications for Policy," *Education Finance and Policy* 2, no. 4 (2007): 395–407.

10. Benjamin Master, Min Sun, and Susanna Loeb, "Teacher Workforce Developments: Recent Changes in Academic Competitiveness and Job Satisfaction of New Teachers," *Education Finance and Policy* 13, no. 3 (July 2018): 310–322; Corcoran, Evans, and Schwab, "Women, the Labor Market, and the Declining Relative Quality of Teachers," 449–470; Corcoran, "Long-Run Trends in the Quality of Teachers," 395–407.

11. Monty Python, "Finland," *Monty Python's Contractual Obligation Album, 1980.*

12. For example, Finland was in the middle of the international pack in the 1962–1967 IEA First International Mathematics Study, 1967–1973 IEA First International Science Study, 1967–1973 IEA Study of Reading Comprehension, and 1977–1981 IEA Second International Mathematics Study.

13. See OECD, *Education at a Glance 2014* (Paris: OECD, 2014), figure 5.6.

14. Charles T. Clotfelter, Helen F. Ladd, and Jacob L. Vigdor, "Teacher Credentials and Student Achievement: Longitudinal Analysis with Student Fixed Effects," *Economics of Education Review* 26, no. 6 (2007): 673–682.

15. Raj Chetty, John N. Friedman, and Jonah E. Rockoff, "Measuring the Impacts of Teachers II: Teacher Value-Added and Student Outcomes in Adulthood," *American Economic Review* 104, no. 9 (2014): 2633–2679.

16. David Deming, "Better Schools, Less Crime?," *Quarterly Journal of Economics* 126, no. 4 (2011): 2063–2115.

17. Interview with Andre Weiss, German Confederation of Skilled Crafts (Zentralverband des Deutschen Handwerks), by Andrew Leigh, Berlin, September 25, 2017.

18. Franziska Hampf and Ludger Woessmann, "Vocational vs. General Education and Employment over the Life-Cycle: New Evidence from PIAAC," *CESifo Economic Studies* 63, no. 3 (2017): 255–269. See also Eric A. Hanushek, Guido Schwerdt, Ludger Woessmann, and Lei Zhang, "General Education, Vocational Education, and Labor-Market Outcomes over the Life-Cycle," *Journal of Human Resources* 52, no. 1 (217): 48–87.

19. Ludger Woessmann, "Vocational Education in Apprenticeship Systems: Facing the Life-Cycle Trade-offs" (Helsinki: Economic Policy Council, 2017).

20. David J. Deming and Kadeem L. Noray, "STEM Careers and Technological Change," NBER Working Paper 25065 (Cambridge, MA: National Bureau of Economic Research, 2018).

21. "Three Years and Score; University Education," *The Economist* 426, no. 9073 (2018): 60.

22. Jaison R. Abel and Richard Deitz, "Do the Benefits of College Still Outweigh the Costs?," *Current Issues in Economics and Finance* 20, no. 3 (2013): 1–11.

23. Seth D. Zimmerman, "The Returns to College Admission for Academically Marginal Students," *Journal of Labor Economics* 32, no. 4 (2014): 711–754. See also Philip Oreopoulos and Uros Petronijevic, "Making College Worth It: A Review of the Returns to Higher Education," *Future of Children* 23, no. 1 (2013): 41–65.

24. "Tuition and Fees, 1998–99 through 2018–19," *Chronicle of Higher Education*, December 31, 2018, https://www.chronicle.com/interactives/tuition-and-fees.

25. Jennifer Ma, Sandy Baum, Matea Pender, and C. J. Libassi, *Trends in College Pricing 2018* (New York: College Board, 2018), 13.

26. Sallie Mae and Ipsos Public Affairs, *How America Pays for College: A Snapshot of the 10th National Study* (Washington DC: Ipsos Public Affairs, 2017), 5.

27. "Q4 2007 Statistics on College Student Drop Out Rates," http://www.duck9.com/College-Student-Drop-Out-Rates.htm.

28. Abel and Deitz, "Do the Benefits of College Still Outweigh the Costs?"

29. Ma, Baum, Pender, and Libassi, *Trends in College Pricing 2018*, 18–19.

30. Abel and Deitz, "Do the Benefits of College Still Outweigh the Costs?"

31. Abel and Deitz, "Do the Benefits of College Still Outweigh the Costs?"

32. Eric P. Bettinger, Bridget Terry Long, Philip Oreopoulos, and Lisa Sanbonmatsu, "The Role of Application Assistance and Information in College Decisions: Results from the H&R Block FAFSA Experiment," *Quarterly Journal of Economics* 127, no. 3 (2012): 1205–1242.

33. Quoted in Institute for College Access and Success, *On the Sidelines of Simplification: Stories of Navigating the FAFSA Verification Process* (Oakland, CA: Institute for College Access and Success, 2016), 7.

34. Joel Best and Eric Best, *The Student Loan Mess: How Good Intentions Created a Trillion-Dollar Problem* (Berkeley: University of California Press, 2014).

35. Bruce Chapman, "Income Contingent Loans in Higher Education Financing," *IZA World of Labor* 227 (February 2016), https://wol.iza.org/uploads/articles/227/pdfs/income-contingent-loans-in-higher-education-financing.pdf.

36. Joshua Goodman, Julia Melkers, and Amanda Pallais, "Can Online Delivery Increase Access to Education?," *Journal of Labor Economics* 37, no. 1 (2019), 1–34.

37. "New Schemes Teach the Masses to Build AI," *The Economist*, October 25, 2018.

38. Dhawal Shah, "Class Central's Zeitgeist: A Year in MOOCS—2017," Class Central, December 14, 2017, https://www.class-central.com/report/zeitgeist-moocs -2017.

39. Dhawal Shah, "MOOC Trends in 2017: Increased Flexibility and Convenience," Class Central, January 8, 2018, https://www.class-central.com/report/mooc-trends -increased-flexibility-and-convenience.

40. Scott DeRue, cited in "The Return of the MOOC; Upstarts and Incumbents," *The Economist* 422, no. 9023 (2017): 9.

41. "A Conversation with Google's Hal Varian," Council on Foreign Relations, February 7, 2018, https://www.cfr.org/event/conversation-googles-hal-varian.

42. Quoted in Steven Leckart, "The Stanford Education Experiment Could Change Higher Learning Forever," *Wired*, March 20, 2012.

43. Maria Konnikova, "Will MOOCs Be Flukes?," *New Yorker*, November 7, 2014; Susan Dynarski, "Online Courses Fail Those Who Need Help," *New York Times*, January 21, 2018, BU3.

44. This section draws on Andrew Leigh, "Why the Battle over Hiring Rival Employees Could Be the Next Big Challenge for Australian Workplaces," *Business Insider*, January 20, 2017, https://www.businessinsider.com.au/why-the-battle-over-hiring -rival-employees-could-be-the-next-big-challenge-for-australian-workplaces-2017-1.

45. David Streitfeld, "Engineers Allege Hiring Collusion in Silicon Valley," *New York Times*, March 1, 2014, A1.

46. Evan P. Starr, J. J. Prescott, and Norman Bishara, "Noncompetes in the U.S. Labor Force," University of Michigan Law and Economic Research Paper No. 18-013, December 24, 2017, https://ssrn.com/abstract=2625714.

47. Matt Marx, Jasjit Singh, and Lee Fleming, "Regional Disadvantage? Noncompete Agreements and Brain Drain," *Research Policy* 44, no. 2 (2015): 394–404.

48. Evan P. Starr, Justin Frake, and Rajshree Agarwal, "Mobility Constraint Externalities," *Organization Science* (forthcoming).

49. Alan B. Krueger, "The Rigged Labor Market," *Milken Institute Review*, April 28, 2017, http://www.milkenreview.org/articles/the-rigged-labor-market.

50. One study uses data from CareerBuilder.com. See José Azar, Ioana Marinescu, and Marshall I. Steinbaum, "Labor Market Concentration," NBER Working Paper No. 24147 (Cambridge, MA: National Bureau of Economic Research, 2017). The other study uses data from three Census Bureau surveys—the Longitudinal Business Database, the Census of Manufacturers, and the Annual Survey of Manufacturers. See Efraim Benmelech, Nittai Bergman, and Hyunseob Kim, "Strong Employers and Weak Employees: How Does Employer Concentration Affect Wages?," NBER

Working Paper No. 24307 (Cambridge, MA: National Bureau of Economic Research, 2018).

51. Suresh Naidu, Eric Posner, and Glen Weyl, "More and More Companies Have Monopoly Power over Workers' Wages. That's Killing the Economy," *Vox*, April 6, 2018, https://www.vox.com/the-big-idea/2018/4/6/17204808/wages-employers-workers-monopsony-growth-stagnation-inequality.

52. Dick M. Carpenter II, Lisa Knepper, Kyle Sweetland, and Jennifer McDonald, *License to Work: A National Study of Burdens from Occupational Licensing*, 2nd ed. (Arlington, VA: Institute for Justice, 2017), 38.

53. Jason Furman, "License to Compete: Occupational Licensing and the State Action Doctrine" (prepared testimony before the US Senate Committee on the Judiciary Subcommittee on Antitrust, Competition Policy, and Consumer Rights, hearing on February 2, 2016).

54. Carpenter, Knepper, Sweetland, and McDonald, *License to Work*, 25, 174.

55. Carpenter, Knepper, Sweetland, and McDonald, *License to Work*, 36.

56. Department of the Treasury Office of Economic Policy, Council of Economic Advisers, and Department of Labor, *Occupational Licensing: A Framework for Policymakers*, July 2015, https://obamawhitehouse.archives.gov/sites/default/files/docs/licensing_report_final_nonembargo.pdf.

57. Peter Q. Blair and Bobby W. Chung, "How Much of Barrier to Entry Is Occupational Licensing?," NBER Working Paper No. 25262 (Cambridge, MA: National Bureau of Economic Research, 2018).

58. Janna E. Johnson and Morris M. Kleiner, "Is Occupational Licensing a Barrier to Interstate Migration?," NBER Working Paper No. 24107 (Cambridge, MA: National Bureau of Economic Research, 2017).

59. Jason Furman, "License to Compete: Occupational Licensing and the State Action Doctrine" (prepared testimony before the US Senate Committee on the Judiciary Subcommittee on Antitrust, Competition Policy, and Consumer Rights, hearing on February 2, 2016).

60. Andrea Kramar and Mary Stevens, "Some of the Strangest Jobs People Have Paid Others to Do on TaskRabbit," *Make It*, CNBC, January 17, 2017.

61. McKinsey Global Institute, *Connecting Talent with Opportunity in the Digital Age*, June 2015, https://www.mckinsey.com/featured-insights/employment-and-growth/connecting-talent-with-opportunity-in-the-digital-age.

62. Seth D. Harris and Alan B. Krueger, *Proposal for Modernizing Labor Laws for Twenty-First-Century Work: The "Independent Worker,"* Hamilton Project Discussion Paper No. 2015–10 (Washington, DC: Hamilton Project, 2015).

63. Harris and Krueger, *Proposal for Modernizing Labor Laws for Twenty-First-Century Work*, 6.

64. Noam Scheiber, "Gig Economy Dealt a Blow by a Ruling in California," *New York Times*, May 1, 2018, B6.

65. These forms of intermediate classifications of workers have solid support in economic theory. See Andre Hagiu and Julian Wright, "The Status of Platforms and Workers in the Sharing Economy" *Journal of Economics and Management Strategy* 28, no. 1 (2019): 97–108 .

66. See, for example, Truman F. Bewley, *Why Wages Don't Fall during a Recession* (Cambridge MA Harvard University Press, 1999); David Card, Alexandre Mas, Enrico Moretti, and Emmanuel Saez, "Inequality at Work: The Effect of Peer Salaries on Job Satisfaction," *American Economic Review* 102, no. 6 (2012): 2981–3003; Emily Breza, Supreet Kaur, and Yogita Shamdasani, "The Morale Effects of Pay Inequality," *Quarterly Journal of Economics* 133, no. 2 (2018): 611–663.

67. Sandra E. Black, Diane Whitmore Schanzenbach, and Audrey Breitwieser, "The Recent Decline in Women's Labor Force Participation," in *The 51%: Driving Growth through Women's Economic Participation*, ed. Diane Whitmore Schanzenbach and Ryan Nunn (Washington, DC: Hamilton Project, Brookings Institution, 2017), 5–18.

68. Ryan Nunn and Megan Mumford, "The Incomplete Progress of Women in the Labor Market," in *The 51%: Driving Growth through Women's Economic Participation*, ed. Diane Whitmore Schanzenbach and Ryan Nunn (Washington, DC: Hamilton Project, Brookings Institution, 2017), 19–32.

69. Claudia Goldin, "A Grand Gender Convergence: Its Last Chapter," *American Economic Review* 104, no. 4 (2014): 1091–1119; Henrik Kleven, Camille Landais, and Jakob Egholt Søgaard, "Children and Gender Inequality: Evidence from Denmark," NBER Working Paper No. 24219 (Cambridge, MA: National Bureau of Economic Research, 2018).

70. Elizabeth U. Cascio, "Public Investments in Child Care," in *The 51%: Driving Growth through Women's Economic Participation*, ed. Diane Whitmore Schanzenbach and Ryan Nunn (Washington, DC: Hamilton Project, Brookings Institution, 2017), 123–142.

71. Christopher J. Ruhm, "A National Paid Parental Leave Policy for the United States," in *The 51%: Driving Growth through Women's Economic Participation*, ed. Diane Whitmore Schanzenbach and Ryan Nunn (Washington, DC: Hamilton Project, Brookings Institution, 2017), 107–122.

72. These events are recounted in Chai Feldblum and Victoria Lipnic, *Select Task Force on the Study of Harassment in the Workplace* (Washington, DC: US Equal Employment Opportunity Commission, 2016), 5.

73. Feldblum and Lipnic, *Select Task Force on the Study of Harassment in the Workplace*, 8, 15–16.

74. Sara LaLumia, "Tax Policies to Encourage Women's Labor Force Participation," in *The 51%: Driving Growth through Women's Economic Participation*, ed. Diane Whitmore Schanzenbach and Ryan Nunn (Washington, DC: Hamilton Project, Brookings Institution, 2017), 71–80.

75. Zvi Eckstein, Michael Keane, and Osnat Lifshitz, "Career and Family Decisions: Cohorts Born 1935–1975," *Econometrica*, 87, no. 1 (2019): 217–253.

76. Goldin, "Grand Gender Convergence."

77. Jodi Kantor, "Working Anything but 9 to 5: Scheduling Technology Leaves Low-Income Parents with Hours of Chaos," *New York Times*, August 13, 2014.

78. Jodi Kantor, "Starbucks to Revise Policies to End Irregular Schedules for Its 130,000 Baristas," *New York Times*, August 15, 2014, A11.

79. Steven Greenhouse, "A Push to Give Steadier Shifts to Part-Timers," *New York Times*, July 15, 2014, A1.

80. On the impact of mandated parental leave on women's employment and earnings, see Christopher J. Ruhm, "The Economic Consequences of Parental Leave Mandates: Lessons from Europe," *Quarterly Journal of Economics* 113, no. 1 (1998): 285–317; Rebecca Edwards, "Maternity Leave and the Evidence for Compensating Wage Differentials in Australia," *Economic Record* 82, no. 258 (2006): 281–297.

81. For more information, see Joshua S. Gans, "Return to Work Credits," in *Paid Parental Leave Policy Brief* (Acton, Australia: Crawford School of Economics and Government, Australian National University, August 2008).

82. "Sanjuana's Story: Earned Income Tax Credit Helps Family Stability," Children First, Communities in Schools of Buncombe County, Asheville, NC, 2014.

83. Jacob E. Bastian and Maggie R. Jones, "Do EITC Expansions Pay for Themselves? Effects on Tax Revenue and Public Assistance Spending" (working paper, University of Chicago, 2018).

84. Hilary Hoynes, *Building on the Success of the Earned Income Tax Credit* (Washington, DC: Hamilton Project, Brookings Institution, 2014).

85. David G. Blanchflower and Andrew J. Oswald, "Well-being over Time in Britain and the USA," *Journal of Public Economics* 88, no. 7–8 (2004): 1359–1386.

86. John F. Helliwell, Richard Layard, and Jeffrey D. Sachs, *World Happiness Report 2018* (New York: Sustainable Development Solutions Network, 2018).

87. Cecil E. Bohanon, John B. Horowitz, and James E. McClure, "Saying Too Little, Too Late: Public Finance Textbooks and the Excess Burdens of Taxation," *Econ Journal Watch* 11, no. 3 (2014): 277–296.

88. Quoted in Thomas Friedman, "While You Were Sleeping," *New York Times*, January 17, 2018, A19.

89. Joseph V. Kennedy, Daniel Castro, and Robert D. Atkinson, *Why It's Time to Disrupt Higher Education by Separating Learning from Credentialing* (Washington, DC: Information Technology and Innovation Foundation, 2016).

90. "The Digital Degree; the Future of Universities," *The Economist* 411, no. 8893 (2014): 20.

91. Section 16600 of the 2010 California Code Business and Professions Code, Chapter 1, Contracts in Restraint of Trade.

92. These proposals draw on Furman, "License to Compete."

93. Bridget Ansel and Heather Boushey, "Modernizing U.S. Labor Standards for 21st-Century Families," in *The 51%: Driving Growth through Women's Economic Participation*, ed. Diane Whitmore Schanzenbach and Ryan Nunn (Washington, DC: Brookings Institution, 2017), 35–56.

94. Laura and John Arnold Foundation, "'Government by Guesswork' Is Not Solving the Nation's Social Problems. A Fundamentally Different—Evidence Based—Approach Is Needed," Straight Talk on Evidence report (Washington, DC: Arnold Foundation, 2018).

95. Andrew Leigh, *Randomistas: How Radical Researchers Are Changing Our World* (New Haven, CT: Yale University Press, 2018).

Conclusion

1. Joseph A. Schumpeter, *Capitalism, Socialism and Democracy* (London: Routledge, 1994 [1942]), 82–83.

2. Quoted in Joe Sharkey, "Reinventing the Suitcase by Adding the Wheel," *New York Times*, October 5, 2010, B6.

3. Ana Swanson, "What People in 1900 Thought the Year 2000 Would Look Like," WonkBlog, *Washington Post*, October 4, 2015.

4. Sendhil Mullainathan, "Get Ready for Technological Upheaval by Expecting the Unimagined," *New York Times*, September 3, 2017, BU3.

5. Bertrand Russell, *A History of Western Philosophy, and Its Connection with Political and Social Circumstances from the Earliest Times to the Present Day* (1946; London: Routledge, 2004), 25; Stephen Fry, *Mythos: A Retelling of the Myths of Ancient Greece* (London: Penguin, 2018). We are grateful to an anonymous reviewer for drawing our attention to this facet of the Promethean myth.

Name Index

Subject Index